THE USBORNE
INTRODUCTION TO
ARCHAEOLOGY
INTERNET-LINKED

These temples, rising through the early morning mist, are located at Bagan in Burma (Myanmar). The site is a gift for archaeologists, as it contains the remains of around 2,000 temples, dating from the 11th to the 13th centuries.

THE USBORNE
INTRODUCTION TO
ARCHAEOLOGY
INTERNET-LINKED

This cave painting from Lascaux, France, has survived for an amazing 17,000 years. It shows a species of wild ox that is now extinct.

THE USBORNE
INTRODUCTION TO
ARCHAEOLOGY
INTERNET-LINKED

Abigail Wheatley and Struan Reid

SCHOLASTIC INC.

New York Toronto London Auckland Sydney
Mexico City New Delhi Hong Kong Buenos Aires

Designed by Neil Francis, Zoe Wray
and Stephen Wright

Archaeology consultants:
Dr. Timothy Taylor and Dr. Norah Moloney

Illustrations by John Woodcock and Ian McNee

Edited by Jane Chisholm

Contents

Archaeology by continent

Archaeology fact file

Handle of a knife made by the Chimu people, who lived in Peru between 800 and 1476. Many similar knives have been found in burials, and may have been used in sacrificial ceremonies.

Internet links

Throughout this book we have recommended websites where you can find out more about archaeology and watch video clips, play games and view interactive exhibits. For links to all the recommended websites in this book, go to the Usborne Quicklinks Website at www.usborne-quicklinks.com and enter the keyword "archaeology".

How to use Usborne Quicklinks

North America

The continent of North America includes Greenland, Canada, the USA, the Caribbean and the countries of Central America. There is a huge range of climates and environments and a rich archaeological record, left by the Native American peoples and by many later visitors and settlers.

Ballpark figures

In 1862, a field worker in the southern Veracruz region of Mexico stumbled across a large stone sticking out of the ground. It turned out to be a colossal sculpture of a head. Years later, several similar heads were discovered nearby at La Venta, which flourished as a religious site between about 1000 and 600BC. Remains of temple pyramids, ball courts and rubber balls were also found there. Archaeologists have named this culture Olmec. The Olmec people played a ritual ball game and marks on the sculpted heads may show the protective helmets the players wore.

This huge sculpted head was discovered at the Olmec site of La Venta. It is more than 2.5m (8 ft) high.

46

The Yukon iceman

The body of a young man was discovered sticking out of melting ice in a glacier in Tatshenshini-Alsek Park, in the Yukon area of Canada, in 1999. Alongside was a squirrel-fur cloak, a hat made of braided tree roots, a walking stick, a spear and various tools. The body was nicknamed Kwaday Dän Sinchi, which means "Long Ago Person Found" in the local language. Radiocarbon dating showed that Kwaday lived around 550 years ago. He was 18 to 22 years old at his death and was probably overcome by cold while trekking across the glacier during a hunting trip.

Waste not, want not

At the University of Arizona at Tucson, archaeologists have been investigating waste since 1973. They sort and study refuse collected from different sources nearby, to find out more about people's use and disposal habits for food and other kinds of products. This may seem surprising, but there are good reasons why these archaeologists have chosen to spend years up to their elbows in filth. Many of the artifacts more traditional archaeologists find are also refuse, thrown away by people many years ago. Studying modern waste helps to explain why and how different things were disposed of in the past.

GREENLAND

To find out more about frozen mummies found here, see pages 18-19.

Qilakitsoq

ALASKA

Tatshenshini-Alsek Park

Viking artifacts have been discovered here; see page 50.

L'Anse aux Meadows

CANADA

Pueblo houses and Native American artifacts can still be seen at Mesa Verde and Chaco Canyon; see pages 48-49.

Mesa Verde
Chaco Canyon
Tucson

UNITED STATES OF AMERICA

Annapolis is the site of some major historical archaeology investigations; see page 30.

Annapolis
Jamestown

Great Serpent Mound

Remains of an early European fort have been found at Jamestown; see page 51.

MEXICO

Tenochtitlan and Teotihuacan were important sites for the Aztec people; see pages 52-53.

Teotihuacan
Tenochtitlan
La Venta
Palenque

HONDURAS

COSTA RICA

THE BAHAMAS

CUBA

Mound builders

Thousands of earth mounds stand along the Mississippi, Ohio and Illinois rivers, which flow from the heart of the USA to the southeast. The most spectacular is Great Serpent Mound, shaped liked a huge snake swallowing an egg. One mound in Virginia became part of America's earliest archaeological dig, when Thomas Jefferson, later to become US President, excavated it in 1784. He found over a thousand skeletons, and realized that the mound had been used for burials by the local Native American people for hundreds of years. Other mounds have revealed artifacts such as copper animal figures and intricate shapes cut from paper-thin sheets of mineral mica. The mounds were probably built between about 300BC and AD500.

This bird's claw shape made of mica is so fragile, its use is a mystery.

Maya mysteries

The temple pyramid at Palenque has stood, surrounded by jungle, since the Maya people built it in the 7th century. It was only in 1952 that Mexican archaeologist Alberto Ruiz Lhuillier realized the temple was also a tomb. He noticed an unusual slab in the temple floor; under which he found stairs leading down inside the pyramid. At the bottom were human remains, sculpted plaster heads; and, further on, a huge carved stone sarcophagus. Maya glyph writing on the sarcophagus reveals that the body inside, its face covered with a delicate green jade mask, was the Maya leader Pacal the Great, who ruled between 615 and 683. He was buried with rich jade ornaments, including rings and necklaces.

This is the Temple of the Inscriptions at Palenque, in Mexico. In 1952, archaeologists were amazed to discover it contained a royal burial.

Internet links

For links to websites where you can find out more about the Olmec ball game and explore a Maya site, go to www.usborne-quicklinks.com

---

1. Look for the "Internet links" boxes on the pages of this book. They contain descriptions of the websites you can visit.

2. In your computer's web browser, type the address **www.usborne-quicklinks.com** to go to the Usborne Quicklinks Website.

3. At the Usborne Quicklinks Website, type the keyword for this book: "archaeology".

4. Type the page number of the link you want to visit. When the link appears, click on it to go to the recommended site.

Internet links

For links to websites where you can find out more about the Olmec ball game and explore a Maya site, go to **www.usborne-quicklinks.com**

The links in Usborne Quicklinks are regularly updated, but occasionally you may find a site is unavailable. This may only be temporary so try again later, or even the next day.

Websites to visit

Here are some examples of the many things you can do on the websites recommended in this book:

- Take virtual tours of famous ancient sites

- Follow ancient artifacts from discovery to restoration

- Examine the remains of early human ancestors

- Try your hand at directing a dig

- See virtual reconstructions of ancient buildings and artifacts

- Read about the latest underwater discoveries

- Try your hand at unwrapping a virtual mummy

- Find out how archaeologists read ancient writings

Net Help

For information and help using the Internet, go to the Net Help area on the Usborne Quicklinks Website. You'll find information about "plug-ins" – small free programs that your web browser needs to play videos, animations and sounds. You probably already have these, but if not, you can download them for free from Quicklinks Net Help. You can also find information about computer viruses and advice on anti-virus software to protect your computer.

Staying safe online

Make sure you follow these simple rules to keep you safe online:

Children should ask an adult's permission before connecting to the Internet.

Never give out personal information about yourself, such as your real name, address, phone number or school.

If a site asks you to log in or register by typing your name and address, children should ask permission from an adult first.

If you receive email from someone you don't know don't reply to it. Tell an adult.

Adults - the websites described in this book are regularly reviewed and updated, but websites can change and Usborne Publishing is not responsible for any site other than its own. We recommend that children are supervised while on the Internet, that they do not use Internet chat rooms and that filtering software is used to block unsuitable material. You can find more information on Internet safety at the Usborne Quicklinks Website.

What is archaeology?

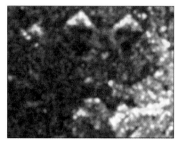

The here are clues to the past all around you, if you know where to look for them. They can be as small as a human hair, or as vast as the pyramids. But, whatever the size, they all help build up a picture of how people lived long ago. This is what archaeology is all about.

The Egyptian pyramids are so huge, they are even visible from space. You can just see them as three triangular blobs in this satellite image.

Leaving a trail

People have always left their mark on the world around them. From prehistoric times right down to the modern era, they have changed the environment to suit themselves, by making tools and homes, producing food and clothing and creating art and monuments. These activities all leave traces, which can sometimes last for hundreds of thousands of years. Archaeologists find and study these remains, to find out as much as they can about how people lived in the past.

Many ancient monuments are still standing, like the famous pyramids of Egypt, built around 2550BC. For centuries these extraordinary structures were a mystery, but archaeologists have studied every inch of them and now know how they were built and who built them.

These holes and trenches were made by archaeologists, digging down to find more clues about how the pyramids were made and used.

Detective work

Clues about the past come in all shapes and sizes. Some are small, carefully crafted objects - known as artifacts - such as tools and clothing, paintings, pots and writings. Others are larger human-made objects, like buildings. The remains of plants and animals that people farmed or ate, and the bodies of people themselves, also preserve many vital clues about their lives.

The remains of tools and buildings show what skills and materials different cultures had, while ancient writings and art give clues about their customs and beliefs. Human, plant and animal remains preserve evidence of diseases and diet, and can show what the climate and environment were like long ago.

World view

Because remains are so varied, archaeology covers a huge range of subjects. History, ancient art and languages, weather and the earth, plants and animals, medicine and diseases, chemistry and physics are all involved. Some archaeologists study just one of these areas, while others search for undiscovered sites and remains.

Archaeologists are uncovering more remains all the time, and using advances in technology to extract even more information. But they will never be able to know everything. The vast majority of ancient objects get lost or destroyed, one way or another, over the centuries. Often the most important things about the past, such as ideas and beliefs, don't leave any traces at all. So archaeologists just have to do the best they can at interpreting what they can find.

Even the smallest remains, like these human hairs, magnified by a microscope, carry traces of chemicals. This helps archaeologists find out about people's health and diet in the past.

Ancient art, like this painting of two boxers from around 1600BC, made by the Minoan people, shows archaeologists what pastimes and fashions people had.

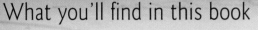

What you'll find in this book

This book takes you through many different archaeological techniques and discoveries. The first section introduces basic archaeological methods and shows how different kinds of remains have survived over hundreds and even thousands of years. The central section looks at world archaeology continent by continent, with features on the most exciting sites and discoveries. The final section explores techniques for dating and reconstructing archaeological remains.

Many of the dates in this book are from the time before the birth of Christ. They are marked "BC", meaning "Before Christ", and are counted back into the past, from the year of Christ's birth. Dates after Christ's birth are counted forwards to the present, and are sometimes marked "AD" for *Anno Domini*, meaning "in the year of our Lord". To read about other dating systems, especially ones used in the past, see pages 94-95.

Surviving through the ages

Very few ancient objects have survived to the present day. That's why the ones that have lasted are so important for archaeologists. But, strangely enough, the same processes that destroy some materials can actually help preserve others. So things that were lost and partly destroyed in the past can survive for the future.

A statue, made by the Maya people more than a thousand years ago, lies on the seabed off Mexico. It was probably thrown into the sea by storms, but underwater it's been protected from harsh winds and human damage.

Internet links

For a link to a website where you can find out more about these processes on a voyage into archaeology, go to **www.usborne-quicklinks.com**

Buried deep

Over time, most things get lost and destroyed by natural weathering and human destruction. People wear out small objects and throw them away, tear down big structures to make way for new ones, and take all sorts of things apart to reuse their materials. They stash away valuables to hide them, and bury refuse and dead bodies to dispose of them safely. Wind, rain, rivers and seas wear away at things, flood them with water, or bury them in sand or soil.

Earthquakes and volcanoes cover them with hot mud or ash. Animals and plants break things up with their teeth or roots, or bury them in the soil or in undergrowth. Layers of mud, sand or sediment build up over time, covering any objects in the way. The ground level gradually rises, so everything buried underneath is lost and forgotten. That's why archaeologists often have to dig deep underground to find things that were once on the surface.

These eggs are more than 1,500 years old. They were discovered in the remains of the Roman city of Pompeii and were preserved by the hot volcanic ash that smothered the entire city in the year 79.

Decaying by degrees

Whether remains are buried, submerged, or just stay on the surface, they almost all start to rot or crumble over time. How things decay - or survive - depends on what they are made of, where they end up and what happens to them over time.

People, plants and animals, and things made of plants or animals, like wood, leather, cloth and bone, are known as "organic" materials. They decay fairly easily. Microbes - tiny living creatures in soil, air and water - eat away at them, causing them to rot.

All other materials - including stone, pottery, metal and glass - are "inorganic". They do not rot in the same way as organic materials, but can crack, corrode or crumble if they are exposed to fire, harsh weather conditions, or certain natural minerals in soil or water.

These processes can take hundreds of years to destroy an object completely. And if something is only partly decayed, that means it's partly preserved, too. Some of it is still there, and there's a chance it may be discovered before it crumbles away.

This ancient Egyptian bronze sculpture of a cat was buried in the ground for more than 2,000 years. Although the metal is pitted and stained, it has survived in one piece since around 600BC.

Lost and found

Even if something has survived for centuries, it is no good to archaeologists unless they are able to find it. Some things, like the Egyptian pyramids, have never been lost, as they have always remained on the surface. Other things, that have got buried underground or submerged underwater, may come to light by chance. Archaeologists can also go looking for remains. But most things are lost for good. That's why the few objects that are found are so rare and fascinating.

It's not just things from the distant past that get lost, found, destroyed and preserved. This process is going on all the time. Even today, the objects and structures we use are constantly wearing out, crumbling, and being thrown away to be replaced by new ones. So, one day, archaeologists of the future will be able to dig down into the ground to discover remains from our time. Next time you throw something away, you could think about how it might survive and what archaeologists of the future might learn from it.

Trash or treasure?

Sometimes, a spectacular treasure emerges after thousands of years, looking almost as good as new. But most finds are damaged and have pieces missing, and many are just ancient junk. For archaeologists, though, it's all priceless.

Time detectives

Everyday objects and the remains of animals, plants and people are just as valuable as ancient gold and jewels for the clues they give about the past. In recent years, scientific tests have been developed for many different kinds of remains, to find out their date and history. But archaeologists get most of their information long before their finds get to the laboratory. They can discover a huge amount by looking at ancient objects in the ground, noting the state and position they are found in. This applies to old bones and pot fragments, as much as buried treasure.

This diagram shows a section through an archaeological site, with layers of deposits from different periods in history. The oldest are lowest down.

872 silver coins were found inside this pot in 1982. Because the coins were carefully put into the pot, archaeologists can tell they were hidden deliberately, not just lost.

Bits and pieces

The state an object is in and the earth and other finds around it are known as its context. Context can give important clues about the object's history, or show how it was used in the past. For example, if fragments of household items are found along with animal bones, they may have been thrown away in a waste dump. If many complete objects are dug up together, they may have been abandoned when people moved away, or buried as a religious offering. Isolated objects may simply have been lost. Human remains with objects arranged around them often indicate a grave.

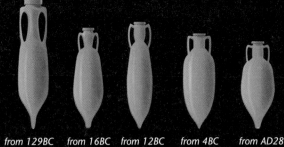

These pottery fragments were broken and thrown away long ago. But their style and location still hold many clues.

This diagram shows how the size and shape of Roman wine storage jars changed over time, based on evidence found at many different sites.

from 129BC   from 16BC   from 12BC   from 4BC   from AD28

Layers and dates

Archaeologists also use context to calculate the date of the things they find. Over time, layers of earth build up on top of one another. The layers farthest down were deposited many years ago, but the top layer, at the surface of the ground, is still forming today. The layers, and any objects trapped inside them, usually stay in this sequence, so archaeologists know that objects and layers lower down are older, while those farther up are more recent. This sequence is known as stratigraphy.

As they dig down, archaeologists look for any changes in soil texture or in the kinds of objects they find, which may indicate the end of one distinct layer and the start of the next. But stratigraphy can be complicated, as layers get disturbed by natural weathering, or by people digging. So archaeologists compare layers and artifacts from different sites, to make sure they have understood their sequence correctly.

Style guide

Archaeologists also compare similar artifacts from different layers and sites, to see how their styles have altered over time, with improvements in technology or changes in fashion. The goal is to build up a timeline for each kind of artifact, showing what styles were popular at different periods. This is known as a typology. It works particularly well for artifacts like pots, which are found in large quantities at a wide variety of sites. New finds, even broken ones, can be matched to the typology, to see what period they are likely to be from.

All this information helps build up a clearer picture of archaeological sites and what's found there. This is what's important to archaeologists - not the financial value of their finds.

This solid gold model boat from the 1st century BC was found in a field in the north of Ireland. The gold is valuable, but the boat is worth far more to archaeologists as evidence of the metalworking and shipbuilding skills of the Iron Age people who made it.

Internet links

For a link to a website where you can see pictures of treasure hoards and play a treasure game, go to **www.usborne-quicklinks.com**

All dried up

Extremely hot, dry places, such as deserts can help preserve things, because there is no moisture there to attract the microbes that cause decay. Even fragile organic remains from plants, animals and humans can sometimes survive for thousands of years in the hottest places. Here you can see some of the most interesting finds from dry sites all around the world.

Mummification

Preserved human and animal remains are often known as "mummies". They can occur naturally in hot, dry conditions and this may have given ancient people the idea of creating mummies themselves. The ancient Egyptians were experts, and some of the people and animals they mummified have survived for 3,000 years with their skin, hair and nails intact.

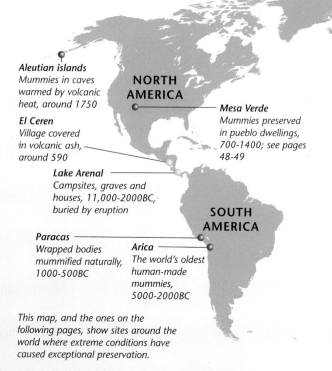

Aleutian islands
Mummies in caves warmed by volcanic heat, around 1750

NORTH AMERICA

Mesa Verde
Mummies preserved in pueblo dwellings, 700-1400; see pages 48-49

El Ceren
Village covered in volcanic ash, around 590

Lake Arenal
Campsites, graves and houses, 11,000-2000BC, buried by eruption

SOUTH AMERICA

Paracas
Wrapped bodies mummified naturally, 1000-500BC

Arica
The world's oldest human-made mummies, 5000-2000BC

This map, and the ones on the following pages, show sites around the world where extreme conditions have caused exceptional preservation.

This mummy was found buried in the sand, seated in a wicker basket, at Paracas in Peru.

Mummies are a mine of information for archaeologists. Their tissues can preserve evidence of ancient health, diet and ways of life. Parasites in the guts of ancient Egyptian pharaohs show that royal sanitation was fairly basic, while all the mummified adults from the American pueblos had osteoarthritis - bone inflammation caused by hard, physical work.

This mummy is from Paracas in Peru and dates from around 1000 to 500BC. It is one of hundreds of mummies from the Paracas culture, which were buried wrapped in elaborately woven textiles and preserved naturally by the hot, arid climate.

Pompeii, Stabiae and Herculaneum
Towns buried in ash, year 79; see pages 86-87

Pylos
Clay tablets, 13th century BC

Taklamakan
Mummies up to 4,000 years old

ASIA

Bogazkoy
Clay tablets, from 16th century BC

Mawangdui
Silk books and bamboo tablets, 3rd century

Qumran
Parchment and papyrus scrolls, 1st century BC

This fragment of a Roman wall painting has survived in almost perfect condition. It was buried at Stabiae in Italy by a volcanic eruption in the year 79.

Akrotiri
Town buried in ash, c.1500BC

AFRICA

Kuk Swamp
Sprinkling of ash on gardens, 7000BC; see pages 62-63

Bahariya Oasis
Huge cemetery of mummies decorated with gold, 3rd century BC

Valley of the Kings
Mummies of the pharaohs, 16th century BC and later

AUSTRALASIA

Oxyrhynchus
Papyrus documents, 1st century and later

Key

- Dried writings
- Mummies
- Volcanic preservation

Internet links

For a link to a website where you can find out how ancient Egyptian mummies were made, go to
www.usborne-quicklinks.com

Dry words

Ancient writings were often made on fragile materials, such as unfired clay, wood, papyrus paper or animal-hide parchment. Although these substances are very vulnerable to moisture, some writings have survived for thousands of years, preserved by the same dry conditions that help mummify bodies. The example below, on papyrus paper, is from an ancient Egyptian tomb.

This scroll of papyrus paper, covered in religious scenes and writings, was found in an Egyptian tomb. The hot, dry conditions that helped mummify ancient Egyptian bodies also preserved the scroll.

Clouds of ash

Volcanic eruptions can cause huge destruction, burning and engulfing anything in their wake. But sometimes they can preserve things too. In ancient Greece, Italy and El Salvador, erupting volcanoes have deposited thick layers of hot ash over human settlements at different periods. The ash kept out air and moisture, and many objects were preserved inside for thousands of years. Archaeologists have dug up amazingly preserved artifacts at all three sites, and have even found some human remains at Pompeii.

Soggy soils

Damp, soggy places, such as bogs and marshes, and the mud at the bottom of lakes, can be very good for preserving organic remains. Many microbes can't survive in these airless conditions, and some environments, such as peat bogs, contain strong, natural chemicals. These can preserve organic remains in just the same way that vinegar pickles food.

This map shows some of the most remarkable discoveries from wet sites around the world.

NORTH AMERICA

SOUTH AMERICA

Ozette
Cloth, hide and wood artifacts buried by mud slides, 16th-20th centuries

Lake Chichancanab
Shells, 750-900

Gatun Basin
Pollen and phytoliths, 9300BC to the present

Windover
Bog bodies with preserved brains, 6000-5000BC

This bog body was found at Tollund Moss in Denmark. He was still wearing a leather hat and the cord around his neck that was used to strangle him.

Bog bodies

Some of the most amazing wet preservation happens in peat bogs, which are made up of rotten vegetation. The acid in peat dissolves in the water and preserves organic remains. Many human bodies have been found in bogs all over Northern Europe, some up to 2,000 years old.

One of the most famous bog bodies is known as Tollund Man. In 1950, two peat cutters working in Tollund Moss in Denmark came across the body of a man, with his hair, skin and internal organs all preserved. Several wounds and a noose around his neck showed he had been killed violently, possibly as a punishment. He was left in the bog around 2,000 years ago.

The only bog bodies found outside Europe are from the wetlands of Florida. The waterlogged soil has preserved everything, even their brains, for up to 8,000 years.

Deep cores

Wet sites preserve vital information about what the weather and climate used to be like. Parts of plants, such as pollen - tiny grains produced by flowers - and microscopic hard cells called phytoliths, can survive for thousands of years. They often sink down to the bottom of lakes, along with small shells and one-celled water plants called diatoms. There they get covered in mud, which builds up over thousands of years.

These remains may sound dull - but they're great for archaeologists. In some lakes, sediment is laid down each year with winter floods, so any remains deposited with them can be dated accurately. Archaeologists count back the layers, year by year, to find out their date. Then they sort the plant and animal matter in each layer to see what different species were present at different times in the past. This gives clues as to whether the region was hot, wet, cold or dry.

Other kinds of remains, such as charcoal from ancient forest fires, can also survive in lake mud. These can be radiocarbon dated, to cross-check the date of the sediment layers.

These are pollen grains, greatly magnified. Each variety of plant produces a different shape of pollen, so archaeologists can identify the species each ancient grain came from.

Somerset levels
Wooden trackway, 3800BC

Oseberg
Wooden ship with leather and textiles, buried 834

Ceide fields
Pollen and fossilized wood, c.5000BC

Novgorod
Many wooden buildings, 10th to 18th centuries

Yde
Bog girl with long hair, 1st century

Tollund Moss
Bog man with surviving clothing, skin and hair, 210BC

ASIA

Lake Suigetsu
Carbon samples, 4300BC onwards.

Lynch's Crater
Charcoal and pollen, up to 135,000 years old; see pages 64-65

near Zurich
Wooden houses and tools from lake villages, 2000BC onwards

Lindow Moss
Parts of two bog men, 1st-2nd century

AFRICA

Key

- Environmental evidence
- Bog bodies
- Waterlogged artifacts

AUSTRALASIA

Lake Naivasha
Fossil diatoms and insects, 1000 to present

Internet links

For a link to a website where you can see pictures and read more about bodies and other things found in bogs, go to **www.usborne-quicklinks.com**

Wet wood

Wood can survive especially well in waterlogged soil. Wooden remains from the world's oldest road have been discovered in a bog in the Somerset Levels of southwest England. The road was built almost 6,000 years ago, from ash, oak and lime planks, and stretched for 1fikm (1 mile).

This wooden sculpture of a whale fin, studded with otters' teeth, dates from 1550. It was discovered in the Native American village of Ozette, trapped under a mudslide.

Archaeologists have also found remarkable wood and bone artifacts at Ozette, a Native American site in Washington, USA. The village at Ozette was covered by mudslides every few years, covering remains dating from the 16th to the 20th centuries. Among the finds were many tools, including fishing nets, wooden looms, canoe paddles, fishing hooks and bows and clubs for hunting. Many of these tools were half-finished, which helped archaeologists find out exactly how they had been made.

17

Icy sites

Extremely cold, wet conditions can preserve things, literally by deep-freezing them, because destructive microbes cannot survive in the icy cold. Dry cold can also freeze-dry remains in the same way as instant coffee, removing moisture by freezing it. Materials that normally decay, such as plant, animal and human remains, can survive for centuries.

This piece from a felt hanging was preserved for 2,500 years in a frozen tomb at Pazyryk in Russia. It shows a reindeer.

Internet links

For links to website where you can explore two different ice mummies, go to
www.usborne-quicklinks.com

Frozen mummies

In the right conditions, cold preservation can be so effective that ancient human and animal remains are almost perfectly preserved. In 1991, two climbers found the body of a man sticking out of ice in the mountains between Italy and Austria. They assumed he was the victim of a modern climbing accident, but radiocarbon dating showed he had in fact lived around 3300BC. His body was so well frozen that his teeth, his skin and the contents of his stomach were still intact. He was named Ötzi, after the Ötztaler Alps where he was found.

At Qilakitsoq in Greenland, several bodies were discovered under a rock overhang in 1972. Six women, a four-year-old boy and a six-month-old baby had all been placed in shallow graves, wearing beautifully made fur and feather clothes and boots. The cold, dry winds and freezing temperatures had preserved everything since the year 1475. Archaeologists could even tell which species of birds and animals the clothes had been made from.

This body of a 6-month-old baby was found at Qilakitsoq, in Greenland. It was preserved by the dry cold for more than 500 years.

Ice and snow cover most of Greenland all year round, creating a permanent freezer, full of microscopic archaeological evidence.

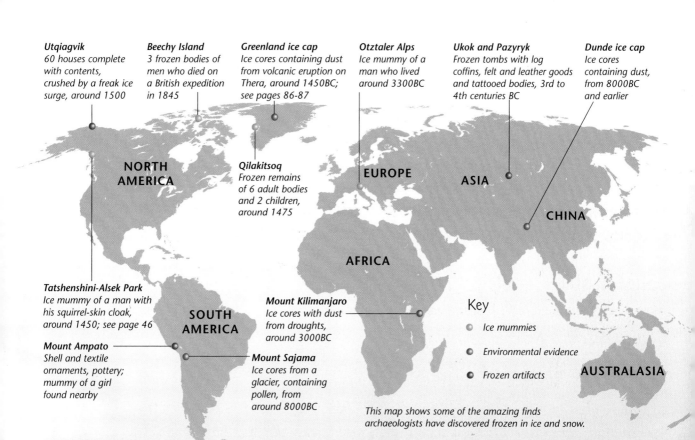

Utqiagvik
60 houses complete with contents, crushed by a freak ice surge, around 1500

Beechy Island
3 frozen bodies of men who died on a British expedition in 1845

Greenland ice cap
Ice cores containing dust from volcanic eruption on Thera, around 1450BC; see pages 86-87

Otztaler Alps
Ice mummy of a man who lived around 3300BC

Ukok and Pazyryk
Frozen tombs with log coffins, felt and leather goods and tattooed bodies, 3rd to 4th centuries BC

Dunde ice cap
Ice cores containing dust, from 8000BC and earlier

NORTH AMERICA

Qilakitsoq
Frozen remains of 6 adult bodies and 2 children, around 1475

EUROPE

ASIA

CHINA

AFRICA

Tatshenshini-Alsek Park
Ice mummy of a man with his squirrel-skin cloak, around 1450; see page 46

SOUTH AMERICA

Mount Kilimanjaro
Ice cores with dust from droughts, around 3000BC

Key

○ *Ice mummies*

◎ *Environmental evidence*

● *Frozen artifacts*

Mount Ampato
Shell and textile ornaments, pottery; mummy of a girl found nearby

Mount Sajama
Ice cores from a glacier, containing pollen, from around 8000BC

AUSTRALASIA

This map shows some of the amazing finds archaeologists have discovered frozen in ice and snow.

Ice sandwich

Ice and snow can also trap evidence of changing environmental conditions. Certain changes in the environment can affect the chemical composition of ice and snow, making them more or less acid, for example. Dust from storms or volcanic explosions, and pollen from plants, is also blown into ice on the surface of the ground.

In very cold places, fresh ice and snow are laid down each year. They trap previous layers underneath, along with the environmental evidence they contain. Scientists drill down into this sandwich of ice to take samples. They can count back through the layers, year by year, to find out when climate changes took place.

Cold comforts

Cold, dry conditions can also preserve artifacts very well. Over the years, many objects, including silver and gold statuettes of people and llamas, have been found scattered on remote peaks of the Andes mountains in Peru. Archaeologists suspect the objects, left by the Inca people, were religious offerings to mountain gods.

In 1929, archaeologists began to excavate burial mounds built around 2,500 years ago at Pazyryk by the nomadic people of the Russian Steppes. The tombs inside the mounds had filled with cold air and water and frozen, preserving felt wall-hangings, wool rugs and leather furnishings, along with coffins containing tattooed bodies.

Watery graves

Water can be a wild, destructive force, but it can also preserve things. Strong underwater currents can quickly bury ships and their contents under a protective blanket of sand. Salty seawater attacks metal, but can help preserve some organic remains.

Sunken ships

The world's seas and oceans cover the remains of thousands of sunken ships. Most just rot away, because wood breaks down quickly underwater, and is often attacked by wood-boring worms; metal parts also deteriorate fast. But the few ships that have survived reveal a huge amount about past shipbuilding. Any cargo that remains also tells archaeologists about trade and navigation techniques. But underwater finds are often very fragile and need careful conservation to preserve them.

NORTH AMERICA

SOUTH AMERICA

Lake Ontario
Two warships, sunk in a storm in 1813

Santa Barbara
Native American camp sites, now flooded. Finds include stone tools, dating to around 1500

Little Bahama Bank
Gold coins, silver bars and coins, bronze cannons and copper pans from a treasure ship wrecked in 1656

Port Royal
City submerged after an earthquake in 1692; houses, tavern and workshops excavated

Titanic Canyon
RMS Titanic, a huge cruise ship, sunk in 1912 after hitting an iceberg; see page 29

In 1961, near Stockholm in Sweden, archaeologists carried out a pioneering underwater excavation. They had located the remains of the *Vasa*, a famous warship that sank on its maiden voyage in 1628. Its intricately carved timbers had survived because of the cold, deep waters where it lay. Marine worms can't live in these conditions, and lack of oxygen prevents decay. After months of underwater excavation and planning, the vessel was raised to the surface. Then a lengthy treatment process began to preserve the sodden timbers by injecting them with hot liquid wax. The *Vasa* is now on display in a specially built museum.

The elaborately carved wooden hull of the Vasa *is one of the most impressive finds ever salvaged by underwater archaeologists. Many artifacts found on board have also been recovered.*

Internet links

For links to websites about the *Vasa* and underwater archaeology, go to **www.usborne-quicklinks.com**

Portsmouth
The Mary Rose warship, sunk in 1545, now raised

Stockholm
The Vasa, an intricately carved warship, sunk in 1628

Cape Riace
2 bronze statues of warriors with coppered lips and silvered teeth, 450BC

Sinan
Chinese trading ship, sunk around 1323 with its cargo of pottery and luxury goods

Although submerged beneath the waves at Cape Riace for more than 2,000 years, this ancient Greek bronze is still in fine condition.

ASIA

EUROPE

Uluburun
Copper ingots, tin ingots and bronze tools from a wreck, around 1300BC

Key

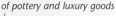 Human settlement

○ Shipwreck

◉ Metal artifacts

Alexandria
City drowned in 4th century; stone statues and parts of buildings discovered

Carthage
Rock-cut port with jetties, around 841-146BC

AFRICA

Port Gregory
Engine of early steamship SS Xantho, sunk in 1882, now restored

AUSTRALIASIA

This map shows some of the most exciting underwater discoveries around the world.

Drowned cities

Historical records from different eras all over the world tell of cities submerged by rising waters or sunk by tidal waves. Recently, underwater archaeologists found parts of the ancient Egyptian city of Alexandria, destroyed by earthquakes in the 4th century. They may even have located fragments of the enormous Alexandria lighthouse, which was one of the seven wonders of the ancient world.

Nearby, the entire ancient Egyptian city of Heracleion, submerged by a natural disaster in the 7th century, has been found. Statues and carvings have been salvaged from Heracleion, including a stone inscription that confirms the city's name.

This head of an ancient Egyptian pharaoh, from 654-525BC, was discovered on the sea bed in the Bay of Aboukir, near Alexandria.

Rusty relics

Metal is especially vulnerable to salty water. Mineral salts in the water often encrust the surface of metal objects and eat away at the structure inside. Sometimes careful conservation can halt this process, but it's rare to find metal artifacts underwater in good condition. Nevertheless, it can happen.

In 1972, a scuba diver saw an arm sticking out of the sand at the bottom of the sea off the southwest coast of Italy, near Riace. Underwater archaeologists were called in and eventually fished out two spectacular, larger than life-size bronze statues. They date back to 450BC and were probably looted by the Romans from an ancient Greek temple. They may have been lost overboard while being shipped back to Rome.

Writing from the past

Ancient writings survive in strange-looking letters on crumbling wood, paper, animal skin or clay, or as inscriptions in stone on buildings and monuments. They can give a fascinating insight into the people of the past, but they aren't always easy to read or interpret.

Ancient records

Written records, also known as texts, often don't last well. In exceptional circumstances, some can survive for thousands of years. But most ancient writings are lost, and many that survive have parts missing, or are written in languages no one now understands. Language experts work hard to translate ancient documents, and have deciphered many mysterious symbols and long-dead languages. But other problems still remain.

A mysterious, 2,000 year old copper scroll, shown above, is an ongoing challenge. It seems to give directions to buried treasure, but no one has managed to locate the places it names, so the treasure has never been found.

This copper scroll was discovered in 1952 in a cave at Qumran, beside the Dead Sea in Israel. It was found with other 2,000-year-old scrolls written in ancient Hebrew, but even experts can't translate all the words.

The inscriptions on this Roman building in Turkey record that it was built in 110, in memory of Celsus Polemeanus, a government official. Written evidence like this provides vital clues about the dating and history of buildings and other artifacts.

The whole truth?

Translation isn't the only problem. We take reading and writing for granted, but they only developed around five thousand years ago. For centuries after that, they were only taught to the rich and powerful, and to a few professional writers, known as scribes.

These people usually wrote down the things which were most important to them, for personal, patriotic, religious or business reasons. So their writings don't always give all the facts. They may distort the truth, or even contain lies designed to show the writer in a good light.

Feathers were attached here

These oval shapes, called cartouches, mark out names.

Dates and places

Language also changes over time, and words and place names get forgotten. But writings can give archaeologists vital clues for finding and dating ancient sites. If a ruler's name appears stamped on a coin or inscribed on a building, archaeologists can guess that nearby objects are from the time of that ruler. Place names also contain clues. Although names of countries, mountains, rivers and cities change, they sometimes keep part of a more ancient place name, or contain a word that hints at an ancient site.

This fan handle, found in an Egyptian tomb, bears the name of the pharaoh Tutankhamun. Inscriptions like this helped archaeologists identify the tomb.

Internet links

For a link to a website where you can try your hand at reconstructing and deciphering ancient writings, go to
www.usborne-quicklinks.com

Old and new

Archaeologists have to deal with many different kinds of ancient writings. Languages, writing systems and the materials they were written on have changed throughout history. The pictures below show just three of the many different forms of ancient writings.

Modern records of all kinds can also be useful to archaeologists. They may include descriptions or pictures of ancient features that have since disappeared, giving useful hints for future archaeological investigations.

A stick with a wedge-shaped end was often used to stamp letters onto the clay.

Cylinder seals were rolled across the clay to print a picture.

Clay tablets were used in Asia from around 3000BC, and later in Europe. Words were scratched or stamped while the clay was wet.

End rod for rolling up the scroll

Jar for ink

Pen cut from a reed

The ancient Egyptians, Romans and Greeks made paper from papyrus plants. They joined sheets to make scrolls, and wrote on them with ink.

Pen made from a quill (feather)

Ink jar made of horn

Knife for sharpening pen

In the middle ages, scribes used prepared animal skin, known as parchment. They wrote on it with inks and paints, and sewed it up into books.

Telltale signs

In this aerial photograph of Stonehenge in Wiltshire, England, vast circular earthworks are clearly visible. They are hard to make out from the ground, but date from 2950BC - 1,300 years before the famous standing stones.

People have always known about ancient sites like Stonehenge and the Great Wall of China, because they have always been visible above ground. Occasionally, construction workers or farmers stumble across unknown, buried remains, when preparing the ground for a building or a new crop. But archaeologists can also go looking for sites, by studying clues above and below the surface of the ground.

Surface clues

Written records from the past may give archaeologists hints about where to look for a site. But they usually need evidence on, or in, the ground to pinpoint a site exactly. Sometimes there are clear signs of something buried, like the stubs of old walls, or small artifacts such as pottery pieces or stone tools poking out of the ground. Archaeologists often survey a possible site just by walking over the ground, noting any small artifacts lying on the surface. If there are a lot, there may be many more below ground.

Bird's eye view

Some sites are difficult to spot from ground level, but maps and photos taken from the air give some clues. Sudden bends in roads may have been made to avoid an ancient structure that has since vanished. Regularly shaped mounds or ditches can indicate human activity. Even buried structures can show up. Stone remains often make the soil around them very dry, while buried ditches create a soggy patch. This is visible in the surface soil, or in crops growing in it. Soil marks and crop marks are best seen from the air.

This aerial photograph shows faint crop marks, caused by buried remains from Roman and Iron Age ditches and walls.

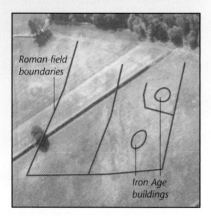

Roman field boundaries

Iron Age buildings

The crop marks are highlighted here to show their shape more clearly.

Seeing underground

Remote sensing technology also helps archaeologists look for buried remains. Portable equipment sends vibrations, or sonar (sound waves) or radar (radio waves) into the ground. These pulses of energy bounce back in different ways, depending on whether they hit something hard or soft. Contrasting materials underground also change the way the soil conducts electricity. Special equipment measures these tiny changes by passing an electrical current into the ground. This is known as resistivity.

Magnetometers don't send out signals, but detect minute magnetic variations by passing electricity through a sealed container of liquid. This reacts to features underground, and is particularly good at detecting remains that have been altered by fire, such as hearths. Simple metal detectors work in a similar way and have been used to locate many important finds by people metal-detecting for fun. All these methods help archaeologists build up a detailed picture of what's hidden under the ground.

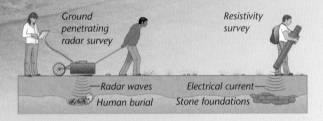

Ground penetrating radar survey

Resistivity survey

Radar waves
Human burial
Electrical current
Stone foundations

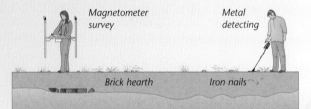

Magnetometer survey

Metal detecting

Brick hearth
Iron nails

Survey from space

Recently, archaeologists have begun to use images from satellites, which combine remote sensing techniques with aerial photography. Methods like these have traditionally been used to detect remains prior to excavation. But archaeologists are increasingly using remote sensing as an alternative to digging. Though it's time-consuming and expensive, it's often less costly than excavation, and gives a clear picture of remains underground without disturbing or damaging them.

Using remote sensing, archaeologists have recently detected the underground remains of a massive Woodhenge near Stonehenge. But they have decided it will be better preserved if they don't excavate it at all.

This satellite image shows ruined temples and enclosures at Angkor, deep in the Cambodian jungle. The satellite "sees" through the undergrowth to the solid structures beneath.

Temple of Angkor Thom

Temple of Angkor Wat

Water channels

Going underground

Digging can reveal a huge amount of information and bring amazing artifacts to light. But it also destroys evidence along the way, and can be very expensive. So archaeologists try to reserve excavation for sites where no other methods are practical, or for rescue archaeology, to investigate things that are about to be destroyed anyway.

Save or destroy?

Excavations uncover many different kinds of archaeological evidence. Small finds such as bone, pottery and coins can be taken away for testing and closer study. Larger objects such as buildings - known as features - may be too big to move, so they have to be left in place, or removed to get at the layer buried underneath. Faint traces of substances in the soil, or outlines of vanished objects, can give clues about remains that have rotted away. These are hard to preserve, but soil samples can be collected for testing and casts made to preserve impressions left by any interesting objects.

Planning stages

The position of objects - their context - is also very important for revealing the original use and date of the site. Unfortunately, context is destroyed the moment things are moved. So it's vital to record everything about a dig as accurately as possible. The site is often divided into squares, to make measuring easier. These diagrams show some of the different ways a dig and its finds can be recorded.

Here you can see how archaeologists lay out a grid for a new excavation. They measure squares and mark them out with stakes and tapes.

This is how finds are recorded - in this case, a human burial. Laser measuring tools are used to record its position before anything is moved.

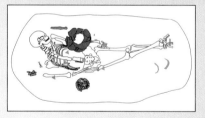

This is a computer drawing, made using information obtained from the laser measuring tool. It shows the whole find in position.

Digging down

When archaeologists dig, they remove the earth carefully, layer by layer. This way they can get an accurate idea of the site's stratigraphy - the relationship of its different levels. This tells them the rough age of each layer and the date of the artifacts they find in it. The depth of finds is very important, so detailed plans and drawings are made, showing the dig site from above and in cross-section.

Moveable finds, like this Roman statue found at Aphrodisias in Turkey, can be taken away to be studied and preserved.

Internet links

For a link to a website where you can excavate a site in an online game to rescue a prehistoric burial, go to www.usborne-quicklinks.com

Tools of the trade

Archaeologists use different tools for different kinds of digging. A mechanical digger may be used to clear large areas where no artifacts are expected. For smaller areas they use little shovels called trowels. But around really delicate artifacts, they have soft brushes and tiny picks to clear away the earth crumb by crumb. But the dig is only the first stage. Once it is over, the archaeologists may spend years testing, examining and comparing all the information they have gathered, back at the laboratory or the library.

This dig is at St. Mary's City, Maryland, a town built by some of the first Europeans to settle in this part of the USA. Archaeologists have dug down to the original floor level - you can see brick floors and the stubs of walls.

Waste earth in this wheelbarrow will be sieved, to check no small finds have been missed.

This archaeologist is using a shovel to dig down to the surface of the brick floor. When it is all laid bare, it will be measured and photographed. Then it will be removed to expose the layer underneath.

The natural edges of features, such as walls or pits, help archaeologists see where one feature stops and another starts. They leave them in place wherever they can.

Note-taking, measuring and recording go on all the way through the dig.

Pits are hollowed out around features that extend down into the ground, to find out how deep they go.

Shapes and sizes

Different kinds of excavation suit different sites. Some sites have many layers, as people lived there for hundreds or thousands of years, piling new buildings on top of old ones. Archaeologists may dig just a few small, deep holes, to see how the site changed over time. Other sites do not have many layers, as people lived there for a shorter period. Here archaeologists clear a wide, shallow area to see how the site was used at one time.

Underwater world

This image of a sunken World War II cargo ship was made using multibeam sonar - a combination of different sound waves.

The ship is lying in two pieces in the Thames estuary, in England. Investigations suggest that a design fault caused the hull to crack. This sank the ship.

These banks and hollows are formed by water currents. They show archaeologists how currents are affecting the wreck.

Wonderful things lie beneath the world's oceans, from ancient shipwrecks and their cargoes to complete drowned cities. Since scuba diving equipment was developed in the 1940s, archaeologists have been able to explore freely underwater. They have developed techniques for recording and, sometimes, salvaging the lost treasures of the deep.

Dangers of the deep

Underwater archaeology can be difficult and dangerous. Some seas have strong currents and can be very rough or cold. Even in good conditions, visibility is poor, and digging disturbs mud and sand, which quickly cloud the water. Diving and underwater surveying equipment is also very expensive. So underwater investigations are often very short, and have to be planned very carefully.

Remote sensing techniques similar to those used on land help archaeologists plan their underwater investigations. Magnetometers detect small differences in magnetic fields and can locate iron objects, such as ship nails or cannons, from 100m (about 300ft) away. Sonar sends sound waves through the water to detect objects above and below the surface of the seabed, with an accuracy of just a few inches. Archaeologists use several of these sensors at the same time, by towing them behind a boat.

Underwater dig

Once an underwater site has been discovered, there are several ways of investigating it. Divers carry video cameras to record images of finds. They also use sonar beacons or satellite-linked global positioning devices to mark the exact location of any finds.

Objects that have been underwater for a long time can be very difficult to preserve on dry land. So underwater archaeologists often decide to leave their finds on the seabed, after recording them carefully. If they decide to remove any artifacts, great care must be taken not to damage them.

A grid helps divers record the position of finds, using drawings, photos or videos.

A suction pipe, called an air lift, sucks up sediment that might cloud the water.

Large finds are floated to the surface in baskets with balloons attached.

This two-seat Deep Rover submersible, named "Jules", operates at depths of up to 2,000m (around 7,000ft). It was used to find a British ship, The Royal Captain, that sank in 1773 in the Philippines.

This viewing bubble is made of acrylic 20cm (8 in) thick, to withstand the water pressure.

These arms can grab finds and samples and carry them to the surface.

Internet links

For a link to a website where you can see underwater pictures of the Titanic, go to **www.usborne-quicklinks.com**

This is the left-hand propellor of the Titanic, photographed from a deep-sea submersible in 1991.

Wet technology

Even the most experienced divers can only get down to about 120m (400ft). To investigate deeper finds, underwater archaeologists use manned submersibles, or unmanned ROVs (remotely operated vehicles), which can take photographs and video footage, and collect archaeological samples. This means archaeologists can now reach sites as far down as 6,000m (20,000ft) deep.

Heart of the ocean

One of the most famous wrecks to be investigated in this way is the *RMS Titanic*, which sank in 1912 after it hit an iceberg. The *Titanic* now lies in icy cold, utterly dark water at a depth of more than 3,800m (12,500ft). But archaeologists using small manned submersibles have managed to locate and investigate the *Titanic*, take photos and videos and even salvage some objects belonging to its unlucky passengers.

Recent remains

Archaeology is often about investigating the ancient past, when very little was written down, and even before writing existed at all. But archaeologists also investigate more recent times, to find out about all the objects and evidence behind the written records. This is sometimes called historical archaeology.

Underground culture

Historical archaeology is especially useful for investigating aspects of life, or people, that didn't make it into the official record. For example, digs in Annapolis, in the USA, have unearthed evidence about the city's black residents in the 18th and 19th centuries.

Beneath the floor of a large house, archaeologists found twelve quartz crystals which had been buried deliberately under an upturned bowl. Historical records show that slaves of African origin lived in this part of the house, so the crystals and bowl were probably *minkisi* - religious objects used by people from West Africa. This find shows the slaves were still following their own religion, though records of the time denied this.

These objects are 18th century finds from Annapolis, USA. They include a toothbrush handle, a clay pipe, a coin, a shard of china and a glass bottle stopper. They all provide archaeologists with details about life at the time.

Internet links

For a link to a website where you can explore archaeological sites at Annapolis, go to **www.usborne-quicklinks.com**

War and industry

Historical archaeology can be as varied as the recent past itself. Recently, interest has been growing in things left behind by the early industrial age, such as factories, mines, bridges, railways and canals. There are plenty of surviving documents about these things, but the actual remains often bring to light unexpected details. Battlefields and equiment from recent wars, like this World War II gunship, can also tell archaeologists a great deal about what really happened in the heat of battle.

These divers are investigating a German torpedo boat, which is slowly decaying where it sank in 1944, off the coast of Croatia. Archaeologists are now recording sites like these.

Historic buildings like these have their own archaeology. This is St. Mark's Basilica in Venice, Italy. Work began on it in 1063, but went on for hundreds of years.

Floods are a constant threat for Venetian buildings, but age also weakens them.

Still standing

A lot of interesting things from the recent past are still visible above ground, so some historical archaeologists don't have to go to the trouble of digging at all. Buildings can reveal a huge amount about the people who made and used them. Churches like St. Mark's Basilica in Venice, Italy, were built over hundreds of years. Often, parts were reused from earlier buildings, or imported from overseas for decorative touches. To track down the history of each part of a building like this, a detailed survey is needed. Archaeologists measure the size,

shape and position of each part of the building and try to figure out how the different parts were put together. They also test samples of the building materials, to discover where they came from, what age they are and whether they have weakened or decayed. This helps them figure out exactly how the structure fits together, and how it has changed over time. It is also useful in monitoring the building for wear and tear and planning repairs. With buildings like St. Mark's, at risk from constant floods, this process is going on all the time.

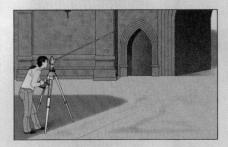

Here you can see how an archaeologist uses a laser measuring tool to measure a building. This is the first stage in creating a record of the building.

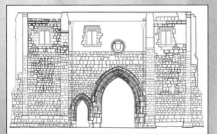

This information is fed into a computer to create a detailed plan like this one. Different shades mark changes in building materials and construction dates.

Living history

There are always gaps in our knowledge of the past, even after the most careful investigations. One way of filling these gaps is by trying out at first hand the kinds of objects and techniques ancient people used. Archaeologists do this by experimenting with modern reconstructions of ancient artifacts, or by studying living people who still use traditional techniques and tools.

Modern stone tools, like these finely worked Australian aboriginal spear heads, are still being made today using ancient techniques.

Skills alive

Many peoples living traditional lifestyles today have skills and customs that preserve clues about ancient skills and ways of life. Some archaeologists, known as ethnoarchaeologists, learn about the past by studying these people and how they live.

Ethnoarchaeologists have found out some unexpected things about stone tools. Many ancient people made stone tools by hitting a rock with another stone or bone. This method produces rough, jagged edges, but some surviving stone tools were so finely shaped, it seemed impossible they had been made this way.

This man from Namibia in Africa is breaking up a large rock, to shape it into stone tools. He is one of the Himba people, who still make and use stone tools for hunting and preparing food.

Modern people who still make stone tools, like the aboriginal people of Australia, often retouch rough edges by pressing on them with a tool made of bone or wood. Ethnoarchaeologists have found pressure marks matching this method on ancient tools. Now they understand how they were made.

Internet links

For links to websites where you can explore Butser Ancient Farm and find out more about Australian stone tools, go to **www.usborne-quicklinks.com**

Trial and error

By building modern replicas of ancient objects, archaeologists can learn about the different materials and techniques people used in the past. This often reveals surprising details they would never have found from studying these things in the museum or laboratory.

This kind of research is known as experimental archaeology. There's a huge range of areas for experimental archaeologists to look into. But, for an authentic experiment, it is vital to use only the materials and techniques available in the past.

Archaeologists have tried making stone tools, building and sailing replica ships and moving huge stones, using ancient techniques to see how these feats were originally managed. Activities as diverse as playing reconstructed musical instruments, cooking from historic recipes, and making things with replica tools all count as experimental archaeology.

Unlike ancient objects, modern replicas can be handled without too much worry about breaking or damaging them. So they are very useful for teaching people about the past.

These diagrams show how replica Iron Age houses, like the ones in the photograph below, are built.

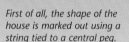

First of all, the shape of the house is marked out using a string tied to a central peg.

Wooden posts are set up, and twigs woven between them to make walls.

A tall central post is erected and rafters are secured to it and the tops of the walls.

The roof is thatched with straw and the walls filled in with mud and straw to keep out the wind and rain.

Living laboratory

An archeological experiment has been going on for 30 years at Butser Ancient Farm in Hampshire, England. It's a working farm, using replica tools and ancient varieties of crops and animals that were farmed in Europe in the Iron Age, around 300BC. Several Iron Age buildings have also been reconstructed, designed to match evidence from excavated Iron Age houses.

The ancient crops grown on the farm have produced much better harvests than expected and the replica buildings have proved very good at keeping out rain and wind.

This suggests that the people of the Iron Age were skilled builders and farmers and had much more comfortable lives than archaeologists used to think.

These reconstructed Iron Age houses at Butser Ancient Farm were built as an experiment, but they also show visitors how people used to live.

Virtual vision

Computers are rapidly becoming one of the most important tools in archaeology. They help make laborious recording work much faster and more accurate. They are also opening up exciting possibilities for computer reconstructions and interaction via the Internet.

This is a virtual reconstruction of the Aztec city of Tenochtitlan, based on remains discovered under Mexico City since 1790.

Internet links

For a link to a website where you can explore Nimrud palace in virtual reality, go to
www.usborne-quicklinks.com

This is the Aztecs' Great Temple. The southwest corner was discovered in excavations in 1913.

This is the temple of Quetzalcoatl, the god of learning. Its foundations were discovered in 1967, during building work for an underground rail station.

This is a ball court, where the Aztecs played ritual ball games. Archaeologists have found similar courts all over Central America.

Virtual view

3-D computer images are incredibly useful for recording existing remains and sites in a way that is easy to use and understand. But it's also possible to make computer images of things that no longer exist, to recreate a virtual view of the past. Using Computer Assisted Design - CAD - archaeologists can create images that reconstruct collapsed buildings, touch up damaged artifacts, or show how they might have looked decorated with painting and sculpture. The images are usually known as virtual reconstructions.

The lost city of Tenochtitlan

The remains of the Aztec city of Tenochtitlan lie buried beneath modern Mexico City. Spanish conquerors destroyed the Aztec city completely in 1521, horrified by the human sacrifices they saw being carried out in the Great Temple. But, since then, remains have gradually come to light, as demolition and building work allow archaeologists to investigate isolated areas of the city.

By studying the scattered remains like this, archaeologists have pieced together a plan of the entire city. It was set on a lake, and divided into four districts. In the central religious precinct were more than 20 temple pyramids. Outside lay Tenochtitlan's royal palaces, with a huge market to the North. This virtual reconstruction, made in 2003, gives a vivid idea of how it would have looked.

Traces of bright wall paintings were found in the remains of the Great Temple, but archaeologists have to guess about the decoration of other buildings, like these temples.

This is the Temple of the Sun. One of its walls was discovered in excavations starting in 1975.

Rebuilding Nimrud

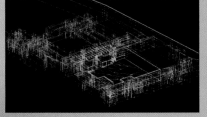

Archaeologists first mark an outline of the floor plan on a grid. They add upright lines to show where the walls are located.

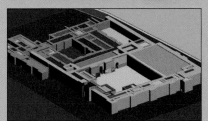

Next, they shade in the solid sections such as walls, leaving rooms and courtyards empty. This is the basic model of the building.

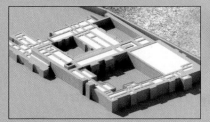

Once the shapes are in place, shading textures and patterns are applied to all the surfaces, and furnishings and people added.

In 1847, the remains of an ancient palace were discovered in modern Iraq. It was built at Nimrud by King Ashurnasirpal II, who ruled the land of Assyria from 883 to 859BC. The beautiful decorations from the palace are now in museums around the world. This virtual model shows how the palace might have looked. Images like this help archaeologists "fly" or "walk" around, to see how things fit together from different viewpoints. As it's all stored on computer, it's easy to update if more evidence comes to light, and there's no damage to the fragile ancient remains.

ARCHAEOLOGY BY CONTINENT

Here you can find out about
archaeological finds from around the
world. Read about the most exciting sites
and discoveries on each continent and
find out how they came to light.

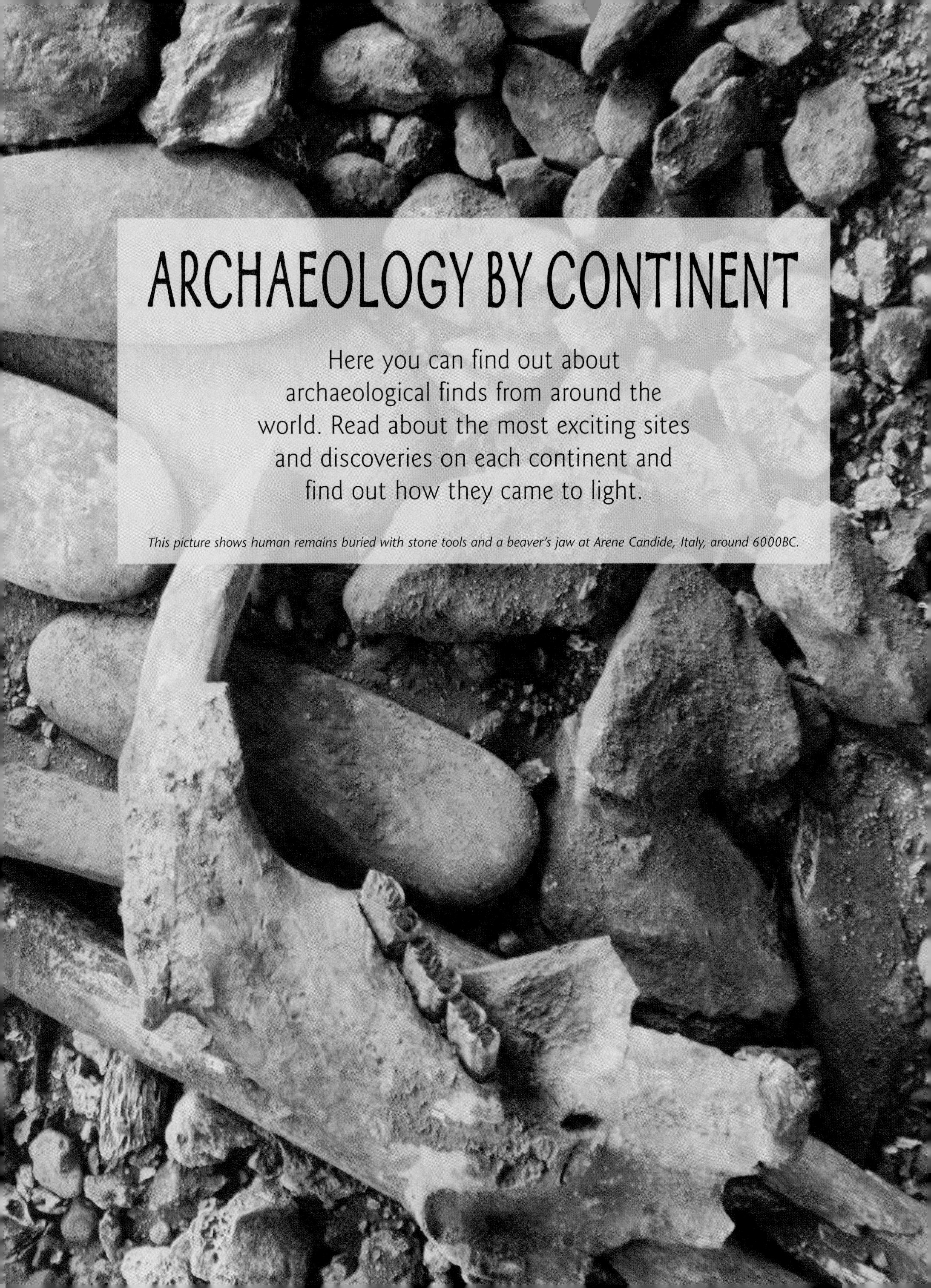

This picture shows human remains buried with stone tools and a beaver's jaw at Arene Candide, Italy, around 6000BC.

Africa

Africa is the second-largest continent in the world, and is made up of 53 different countries. Its archaeology is also vast and varied, beginning with the very origins of human life. Remains range from spectacular sculptures by African artists to the massive monuments of ancient Egypt, and include artifacts and buildings left by the Phoenicians, Greeks and Romans as well.

MOROCCO
Carthage
TUNISIA
Leptis Magna
ALGERIA
LIBYA
MAURITANIA
MALI
NIGER
GUINEA
NIGERIA
Nok
IVORY COAST
Ife
Igbo-Ukwu
GABON

This bronze ram's head was unearthed at Igbo Ukwu. It dates from the 9th century - very early for such intricate metalwork.

Spectacular sculpted heads have been found at Nok and Ife; see pages 44-45.

Buried bronzes

In 1938, a farmer digging a water tank uncovered a number of intriguing bronze objects at Igbo Ukwu, in present-day Nigeria. Full excavations in 1959-1960 found the grave of an important chief, who had lived around 1,200 years ago, in the 9th century. The remains of five attendants were found in an upper chamber, and in the main chamber was the chief, seated on a stool and surrounded by ivory tusks, a crown and thousands of glass beads. More intricately cast bronze sculptures were discovered nearby.

House of the chief

The huge, curved stone enclosure standing in open countryside in Zimbabwe is known as Great Zimbabwe and helped give the entire country its name. Archaeologists were puzzled as to who had built it, but recently, many carefully crafted stone structures have been identified in the area, built by the local Shona people from around 900 onwards. *Zimbabwe* means "house of the chief" in the Shona language. The great enclosure was inhabited from about 1100 to 1500, and was the capital of the Shona empire.

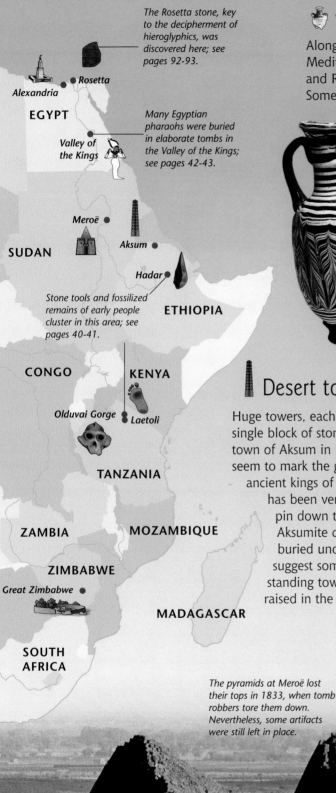

The Rosetta stone, key to the decipherment of hieroglyphics, was discovered here; see pages 92-93.

Rosetta

Alexandria

EGYPT

Many Egyptian pharaohs were buried in elaborate tombs in the Valley of the Kings; see pages 42-43.

Valley of the Kings

Meroë

Aksum

SUDAN

Hadar

Stone tools and fossilized remains of early people cluster in this area; see pages 40-41.

ETHIOPIA

CONGO

KENYA

Olduvai Gorge   **Laetoli**

TANZANIA

ZAMBIA   **MOZAMBIQUE**

ZIMBABWE

Great Zimbabwe

MADAGASCAR

SOUTH AFRICA

The pyramids at Meroë lost their tops in 1833, when tomb robbers tore them down. Nevertheless, some artifacts were still left in place.

Northern powers

Along the north coast of Africa lie remains left by Mediterranean peoples, including the Phoenicians, Greeks and Romans, who settled there over 2,000 years ago. Some columns still stand in the city of Carthage, founded around 814BC by the Phoenicians, a trading people from the east coast of the Mediterranean. There are Roman temples, aqueducts and theatres in many places, but some of the most spectacular standing remains are in the town of Leptis Magna. The city of Alexandria, founded by Alexander the Great in 332BC, has some spectacular Greek remains, including the sunken fragments of a huge lighthouse, one of the seven wonders of the ancient world.

Patterned glass pots, like this one, have been found at sites all around the Mediterranean and North Africa. They were made and traded by the Phoenicians.

Desert towers

Huge towers, each carved from a single block of stone, stand in the town of Aksum in Ethiopia. They seem to mark the graves of the ancient kings of Aksum, but it has been very difficult to pin down their date. Aksumite coins found buried underneath suggest some of the standing towers were raised in the 4th century.

Mini pyramids

Far up the Nile, at Meroë in the northern desert of Sudan, stand several small, elegant pyramids. They mark the tombs of Meroë's kings, and were built between 280 and 350. The tombs have been robbed, but some still contained weapons, wooden furniture, wall paintings, glass containers and pottery, when archaeologists investigated them in the 20th century.

Internet links

For a link to a website where you can read more about ancient Africa, go to **www.usborne-quicklinks.com**

Early people

Scientists believe all modern humans are descended from early people who lived in Africa hundreds of thousands of years ago. Their remains have mostly crumbled to dust over time. But some incredibly early evidence has survived - from stone tools to fossilized skeletons and footprints miraculously preserved in ancient mud.

Heavily built Australopithecus, lived around 2 million years ago

Becoming a fossil

Remains of plants, animals and people sometimes get buried quickly by many layers of earth, before they rot away. Under the great weight of earth, over millions of years, they gradually turn into rock. Things preserved in this way are called fossils.

Fossilized remains of early people only occur in rocks which were forming at the same time that the ancestors of modern humans were living. Many of the rocks running through Ethiopia into Kenya and Tanzania, and also in South Africa, were forming at just the right time. Specialized archaeologists, known as palaeoanthropologists, started looking for fossils of early people there early in the 20th century.

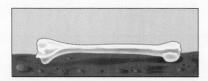
When people or animals die, their flesh usually rots away fairly quickly, but their bones often survive for many years.

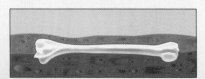
Sometimes, the bones get covered with soil, mud or sand before they decay. More layers of earth gradually build up on top.

The weight of earth pressing down slowly changes the structure of the lower layers, turning both the earth and the bone into rock.

Fossil hunting

In 1959, Olduvai Gorge in Tanzania suddenly came to fame as a site for fossilized remains of early people. Archaeologist Mary Leakey was out walking her dogs there when, purely by chance, she spotted part of a fossil skull in the ground. Once she had excavated it with her husband Louis, palaeoanthropologists examined the skull and discovered it was almost 2 million years old. It belonged to an early, heavily built relative of modern humans, whose scientific name is *Australopithecus boisei*. But the skull was nicknamed "Nutcracker man", because of its hefty jaws.

Even older remains came to light in 1974, in Ethiopia's Afar Desert. Fossil remains on the ground caught the eye of two palaeoanthropologists. Excavation revealed hundreds of fossilized bone fragments from the skeleton of a female. She was another early relative of humans, over 3 million years old, and was nicknamed Lucy, though her technical name is *Australopithecus afarensis*. Lucy's leg bones show she walked upright, like modern people. The development of her teeth suggests she was in her late teens or early twenties, but she was lightly built and only 1.1m (3ft, 5 in) tall.

Fossilized bones, like these skulls from Kenya, vary in shape and size. This helps palaeoanthropologists find out how these different early people were related to each other, and to us.

Homo erectus, lived between 1.8 million and 250,000 years ago

Lightly built Australopithecus, lived around 2-3 million years ago

Tools and traces

This part of Africa held other surprises, too. In 1976 a young archaeologist, working on excavations at Laetoli in Tanzania, noticed a set of footprints on the ground. They turned out to be the fossilized footprints of a group of early people, from nearly 4 million years ago. The footprints show that an adult and a smaller person, possibly a child, walked along together. But the shape of the footprints also proves that these early relatives of humans could walk upright even earlier than Lucy.

Many early stone tools have also been found at Olduvai Gorge and at Hadar in Ethiopia. Some date from around 2 million years ago, which makes them amongst the oldest tools ever found. They were made by chipping pebbles to make sharp edges, and were probably used for cutting and scraping.

These tools, found at Olduvai Gorge, were made between 1.5 million and 150,000 years ago.

Some archaeologists think that this kind of environment, the flat African savannah, first encouraged early people to walk upright to hunt animals.

Internet links

For a link to a website where you can see more fossilized bones of early people, go to **www.usborne-quicklinks.com**

Valley of the Kings

There are so many spectacular remains from the civilization of ancient Egypt that some archaeologists study nothing else. Over the years they have found everything imaginable, from mummies, writings, food, ornaments and furniture to huge temples, luxurious royal tombs and workmen's villages.

This map shows some of the most important ancient Egyptian sites.

This wall painting from Tutankhamun's tomb shows the pharaoh's funeral ceremony. Paintings and inscriptions help show who was buried in which tomb.

Internet links

For a link to a website where you can explore the Valley of the Kings using an online interactive atlas, go to **www.usborne-quicklinks.com**

The glorious dead

Some of the most spectacular discoveries in Egypt have been made in the Valley of the Kings. It's named after the Egyptian pharaohs, who made their tombs there, near their capital at Thebes, from about 1500 to 1000BC. Most of the tombs have been plundered by robbers over the centuries, though impressive wall paintings and inscriptions remain.

But, in 1922, a British archaeologist named Howard Carter discovered a tomb the robbers hadn't found. It belonged to Tutankhamun, a pharaoh who had died suddenly when he was only 18 years old. Carter spent six years searching for the tomb, by making test trenches in different places. Just as his funding was about to run out, he struck gold - literally. Tutankhamun was buried with few goods compared to other pharaohs, but his jewels, gilded furniture and statues, and particularly his golden coffin, have astonished the world ever since.

Many of the pharaohs' tomb workers were buried in this graveyard, above Deir el Medina village in the Valley of the Kings.

Mapping project

Today, archaeologists have more systematic ways of looking for lost tombs. For the last forty years, the Theban Mapping Project has been mapping the whole area of the Valley of the Kings, using remote sensing techniques. The team found a lost tomb in this way in 1995. It's known as KV5, and was built as a last resting place for the sons of Ramesses II.

Unfortunately, tomb robbers cleaned out all the grave goods centuries ago. But it was still a great find. It is the largest tomb ever found in the valley. The plan below shows the huge number of chambers and passageways that have been found so far, but work is still going on, uncovering more rooms and corridors cut deep into the rock.

Some of the wall paintings from Tutankhamun's tomb are splashed with paint - possibly a sign they were finished in a hurry. Archaeologists think the tomb was originally intended for someone else.

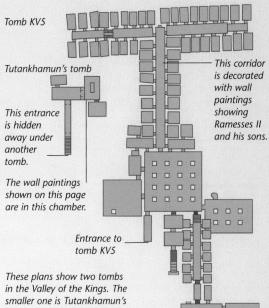

Tomb KV5

Tutankhamun's tomb

This entrance is hidden away under another tomb.

The wall paintings shown on this page are in this chamber.

This corridor is decorated with wall paintings showing Ramesses II and his sons.

Entrance to tomb KV5

These plans show two tombs in the Valley of the Kings. The smaller one is Tutankhamun's tomb. KV5 is shown alongside to give an idea of its size, though it's actually about 45m (150ft) to the Northwest.

Man power

For years, archaeologists searched for evidence of the workers who built the pharaohs' tombs. Finally, in 1929, they identified the village where the workers lived. Deir el Medina village was abandoned around 1080BC, though workshops, houses and shrines survive. But in the workers' tombs archaeologists found many personal possessions, including wigs, boardgames, furniture and cosmetic jars. Sketches and notes for the royal tomb decorations were also found, along with tools and minerals for making paints used in the pharaohs' tombs.

Nigerian art

The country of Nigeria, on Africa's west coast, has seen some of the most exciting discoveries of ancient art ever made. Finds over the last 100 years demonstrate that ancient technology and trading systems in West Africa were far more sophisticated than anyone expected.

Discovery at Nok

In 1928, a baked clay sculpture of a head was found at a village called Nok in central Nigeria, during excavations for a tin mine. Over the next few years, more and more clay sculptures turned up in the area. Few guessed at the time they would prove to be the earliest baked clay artworks ever found south of the Sahara. Archaeologists carried out a dig in 1943 to investigate. Radiocarbon dating of several sites, and thermoluminescence dating of the clay itself, showed that the sculptures were made between 500BC and AD200. The sculptures, and the people who made them, were both called Nok after the site of the first find.

New technology

The discovery of the Nok sculptures has led to further discoveries about the people who made them. Looking at the sculptures, archaeologists can tell they were baked in open ovens, to make the clay hard. Digs at Nok sites have also revealed the remains of more sophisticated furnaces, used for processing iron to make into tools. Before this discovery, archaeologists thought iron smelting technology didn't exist at this period in West Africa. Nok expertise in firing clay must have helped in developing metalworking techniques.

This Nok sculpture is a complete figure. In many cases, the bodies have broken off, leaving only the heads for archaeologists to find.

Camel trains like this one have been trading essential goods across the Sahara for centuries. Archaeologists think these routes helped spread new technology to ancient West Africa.

The headdress on this Ife sculpture may indicate that it is a portrait of a leader. It may also have helped the sculptors disguise marks left by the casting process.

The Ife culture

Baked clay sculpted heads of a very different style were discovered in 1911 at Ife, in southern Nigeria. Thirty years later, brass heads and sculptures in the same style were also found there. They were made between the 12th and 14th centuries, and their serene, lifelike style is quite distinct from any other kind of African art. Careful study of the metalwork has revealed how sophisticated the technology and trade connections of Ife were. Ife sculptors used the complex "lost wax" technique, also known at nearby Igbo Ukwu in the 10th century.

Internet links

For a link to a website where you can explore more Nok and Ife sculptures, go to **www.usborne-quicklinks.com**

Trading knowledge

Lost wax sculptures are difficult to make, as you can see from the diagrams below. So how did a small pocket of West African peoples find out how to make them around this period? The clues lie in the metal. Tests show that the copper in Ife brass came from the distant Sahara region of Africa. Ife metalworkers probably got their copper via the established trade routes of the time, which carried goods across the Sahara. Knowledge of lost wax metalworking techniques may also have passed along these trade routes from cultures farther east.

Ife sculptors shaped a head in wax, and fixed a wax cup and pipes to the top.

They covered the wax in clay and fired it, to harden the clay and melt away the wax.

They poured molten brass into the bowl and down the pipes, into the hollow head.

They broke away the clay and cut off the bowl and pipes to reveal a brass cast of the wax head.

North America

The continent of North America includes Greenland, Canada, the USA, the Caribbean and the countries of Central America. There is a huge range of climates and environments and a rich archaeological record, left by the Native American peoples and by many later visitors and settlers.

Ballpark figures

In 1862, a field worker in the southern Veracruz region of Mexico stumbled across a large stone sticking out of the ground. It turned out to be a colossal sculpture of a head. Years later, several similar heads were discovered nearby at La Venta, which flourished as a religious site between about 1000 and 600BC. Remains of temple pyramids, ball courts and rubber balls were also found there. Archaeologists have named this culture Olmec. The Olmec people played a ritual ball game and marks on the sculpted heads may show the protective helmets the players wore.

The Yukon iceman

The body of a young man was discovered sticking out of melting ice in a glacier in Tatshenshini-Alsek Park, in the Yukon area of Canada, in 1999. Alongside was a squirrel-fur cloak, a hat made of braided tree roots, a walking stick, a spear and various tools. The body was nicknamed Kwaday Dän Sinchi, which means "Long Ago Person Found" in the local language. Radiocarbon dating showed that Kwaday lived around 550 years ago. He was 18 to 22 years old at his death and was probably overcome by cold while trekking across the glacier during a hunting trip.

Waste not, want not

At the University of Arizona at Tucson, archaeologists have been investigating waste since 1973. They sort and study refuse collected from different sources nearby, to find out more about people's use and disposal habits for food and other kinds of products. This may seem surprising, but there are good reasons why these archaeologists have chosen to spend years up to their elbows in filth. Many of the artifacts more traditional archaeologists find are also refuse, thrown away by people many years ago. Studying modern waste helps to explain why and how different things were disposed of in the past.

ALASKA

● Tatshenshini-Alsek Park

CANADA

Pueblo houses and Native American artifacts can still be seen at Mesa Verde and Chaco Canyon; see pages 48-49.

Mesa Verde ●
Chaco Canyon ●

● Tucson

MEXICO

This huge sculpted head was discovered at the Olmec site of La Venta. It is more than 2.5m (8 ft) high.

GREENLAND

To find out more about frozen mummies found here, see pages 18-19.

Qilakitsoq

Viking artifacts have been discovered here; see page 50.

L'Anse aux Meadows

UNITED STATES OF AMERICA

Annapolis is the site of some major historical archaeology investigations; see page 30.

Annapolis

Great Serpent Mound

Jamestown

Remains of an early European fort have been found at Jamestown; see page 51.

Tenochtitlan and Teotihuacan were important sites for the Aztec people; see pages 52-53.

THE BAHAMAS

CUBA

Teotihuacan
Tenochtitlan

La Venta · Palenque

HONDURAS

COSTA RICA

Internet links

For links to websites where you can find out more about the Olmec ball game and explore a Maya site, go to **www.usborne-quicklinks.com**

Mound builders

Thousands of earth mounds stand along the Mississippi, Ohio and Illinois rivers, which flow from the heart of the USA to the southeast. The most spectacular is Great Serpent Mound, shaped liked a huge snake swallowing an egg. One mound in Virginia became part of America's earliest archaeological dig, when Thomas Jefferson, later to become US President, excavated it in 1784. He found over a thousand skeletons, and realized that the mound had been used for burials by the local Native American people for hundreds of years. Other mounds have revealed artifacts such as copper animal figures and intricate shapes cut from paper-thin sheets of the mineral mica. The mounds were probably built between about 300BC and AD500.

This bird's claw shape made of mica is so fragile, its use is a mystery.

Maya mysteries

The temple pyramid at Palenque has stood, surrounded by jungle, since the Maya people built it in the 7th century. It was only in 1952 that Mexican archaeologist Alberto Ruiz Lhuillier realized the temple was also a tomb. He noticed an unusual slab in the temple floor, under which he found stairs leading down inside the pyramid. At the bottom were human remains, sculpted plaster heads, and, further on, a huge carved stone sarcophagus. Maya glyph writing on the sarcophagus reveals that the body inside, its face covered with a delicate green jade mask, was the Maya leader Pacal the Great, who ruled between 615 and 683. He was buried with rich jade ornaments, including rings and necklaces.

This is the Temple of the Inscriptions at Palenque, in Mexico. In 1952, archaeologists were amazed to discover it contained a royal burial.

Pueblos of the Southwest

At Mesa Verde and Chaco Canyon in southwestern USA, stacks of flat-roofed rooms cling precariously to the cliffs. Native Americans in this area used this type of housing, known as *pueblo*, for thousands of years. But the sites had no official protection, and, in the late 19th century, many were stripped of the artifacts left behind by their original builders. Nevertheless, the bare bones of the pueblos still tell a rich and detailed story.

These shell and turquoise ornaments were made by the pueblo builders. Treasure hunters sold off many similar artifacts found in the pueblos.

Bristlecone pine trees from southwestern USA, like this one, have helped experts date wood from the pueblos, by tree ring dating.

Ranger turned rustler

In 1888, Richard Wetherill, a cattle ranger, stumbled across the abandoned pueblos of Mesa Verde. He found room after room of decorated pots, turquoise ornaments and even the mummified bodies of people who had lived there. Wetherill made his fortune selling off the finds and, in 1895, he started to strip the nearby pueblos of Chaco Canyon.

In 1906-7, the American government made Mesa Verde and Chaco Canyon protected National Parks. By this time, little remained apart from the buildings. But archaeologists have recovered a lot of information about the date of the pueblos, the functions of different rooms, and about the builders themselves. For example, investigation of underground rooms, known as *kivas*, has revealed how they were made and how they might have been used.

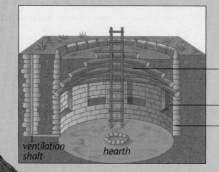

ventilation shaft

hearth

This diagram shows a kiva, an underground room found at many pueblos. This kiva has been cut away to show inside.

The roof was made of pine or fir logs stacked on top of each other. Access was by a ladder through the roof.

Seats were set into the walls

Turquoise and beads were hidden in the walls of some kivas. They may have been religious offerings of some kind, and suggest kivas may have been used for religious ceremonies.

Tree ring dating

Surviving wood from structures such as kivas has provided vital clues about the date of the pueblos. A scientist named Andrew E. Douglass spent a long time studying this wood. By 1930, he realized that he could measure the growth rings made every year by the tree, to give a date when the tree was felled. He discovered that the earliest parts of the pueblos were more than a thousand years old.

Tree ring dating is now a vital archaeological tool, known as dendrochronology. Archaeologists have now used the long-lived bristlecone pine species of the southwest USA to build up a sequence of tree ring dates for this region going back 7,000 years.

Climate change

Douglass also realized that the width of the tree rings could give clues about local climate. He discovered that a severe drought had hit the area just before 1250. Building stopped at the pueblos shortly after this, as the people could no longer live there.

Some pueblos have now been closed, as descendants of the pueblo builders don't like the sites to be disturbed. This is also an effective way of preserving the sites from damage.

This is a pueblo at Mesa Verde in Colorado. There are about 600 dwellings like these at the site.

Internet links

For links to websites where you can find out more and explore a virtual kiva, go to **www.usborne-quicklinks.com**

The round pits you can see at this pueblo are the remains of kivas. Wooden supports from kivas and other buildings helped archaeologists date the pueblos.

The New World

After Christopher Columbus sailed successfully from Spain to the West Indies in 1492, Europeans quickly began to explore and colonize America. They called it the New World, and saw it as a place of untapped riches, legends and possibilities. But archaeology has helped show that Europeans had reached America hundreds of years before Columbus set sail.

Viking copper alloy pins like these helped date the L'Anse aux Meadows site to the 11th century.

Leif and his legend

Ancient Viking sagas tell of Leif Eriksson, an explorer who sailed west from Greenland in northern Europe a thousand years ago and settled in a place he named Vinland. Experts were convinced that Leif had reached Newfoundland in North America, but archaeological evidence for Viking settlement was hard to find. Some artifacts emerged, but they all turned out to be forgeries.

Then, in 1961, excavations began on a group of low, grassy mounds at L'Anse aux Meadows on the Newfoundland coast. The mounds were the remains of eight traditional Viking buildings, made of wooden frames topped with turf. Archaeologists uncovered houses with several rooms, a workshop and even a smithy for metalworking.

Hard evidence

A few small artifacts discovered at L'Anse aux Meadows, including pins and a tool for sharpening needles, confirmed that Viking women had been there, showing that the settlement was a permanent base, rather than a temporary camp used on a raiding trip. These artifacts also helped date the settlement to the years between 1000 and 1020: an astonishing five hundred years before Christopher Columbus set out on his famous voyage of discovery. But the scarcity of finds seems to confirm hints in the sagas that the Vikings left America soon after they arrived.

This replica Viking longship sailed from Greenland to L'Anse aux Meadows in the year 2000, to recreate the voyage made by the first Viking settlers. The captain was a direct descendant of Leif Eriksson.

New beginnings

In 1607, the first permanent English colony in North America was established at Jamestown in Virginia. Among the leaders of the settlers was Captain John Smith, whose friendship with a Native American girl, Pocahontas, has become legendary.

Many modern stories of Pocahontas are very far-fetched. But even the surviving writings from the period, including those by John Smith himself, are very contradictory and confusing. They don't always give a reliable picture of what the early settlement was like. But archaeologists have been investigating the Jamestown site, to try and piece together the facts behind the legends.

Internet links

For links to websites where you can find out more about Viking voyages and Jamestown, go to **www.usborne-quicklinks.com**

Parts of the Jamestown settlement have now been reconstructed to show visitors what it would have looked like. The appearance and layout of these buildings are based on archaeological finds.

Pocahontas and her people

It was thought that all traces of the settlers' first fort on the banks of the James river had washed away. But excavations since 1994 have shown that, in fact, very little of the site has been lost into the river. Archaeologists have located the outline of the huge triangular log enclosure, along with many of the individual holes for the wooden stakes of the palisade. They have also found the impressions of several buildings, two human graves with skeletons still in place and thousands of small artifacts.

The finds have helped give a more reliable picture of relations between the settlers and the local Powhatan tribe, which Pocahontas belonged to. There was some conflict between the Europeans and Native Americans, and the fort was constructed to keep the settlers safe. But artifacts discovered on the site of the fort show that trade flourished between the two peoples. European glass beads and copper were given to the Powhatan people and pottery and much-needed food were given in return.

Hundreds of blue European beads, including these ones, have been found at Jamestown. John Smith recorded that he traded blue beads with the Powhatan tribe, for food.

Aztec archaeologists

The people known as the Aztecs were some of the earliest archaeologists of the Americas. For many years, they wandered Central America, looking for a place to settle. On their travels, they became fascinated by the ancient monuments they found, and investigated them by digging into them and retrieving artifacts. Later, when they settled at Tenochtitlan around 1325, they used their archaeological discoveries as a basis for their own arts, religion and culture.

The massive Pyramid of the Sun at Teotihuacan is surrounded by the remains of ball courts and priests' houses. Modern excavations have been going on at this site for more than a hundred years, unearthing statues, masks and other artifacts, as well as the buildings themselves.

Teotihuacan

Teotihuacan, not far from present-day Mexico City, was a great city and religious site which flourished from the 1st century to around 750. It was laid out on a neat grid plan, dominated by a main street known as the Avenue of the Dead, and two huge pyramids - temples of the Sun and Moon. There were around 600 pyramids of different sizes, as well as houses, workshops and courts for ball games.

Teotihuacan fascinated many Central American peoples, such as the Toltecs, before the Aztecs arrived there. In 1971, archaeologists made a discovery that helped explain why. They found an ancient cave beneath the Pyramid of the Sun, originally created by volcanic lava, but hollowed out and used for religious rituals long before the city was built. This cave seems to have featured in ancient legends as the setting for an important ritual. It was where the gods were thought to have given themselves as sacrifices to create the Sun and Moon and set them moving across the sky.

Sacrifices to the Sun

Teotihuacan had been deserted for centuries before the Aztecs arrived. But they dug into the ancient city to find out more. They were so impressed by the architecture and legends of Teotihuacan that they incorporated them into their culture, along with elements from the Toltec and Olmec cultures. It was probably the legend of the Sun and Moon from Teotihuacan that encouraged the Aztecs to perform human sacrifices, to keep the Sun on its course.

The Aztec culture, and its great capital city of Tenochtitlan, was crushed in 1521 by Spanish invaders known as conquistadors, meaning "conquerors". They were disgusted at human sacrifices they saw being carried out at the Aztecs' Great Temple and attempted to raze the whole city to the ground. But archaeologists keep finding relics of the Aztec capital, buried beneath present-day Mexico City.

This is one of many surviving Aztec masks made of turquoise, a semi-precious stone found in this area. The design echoes masks made by earlier peoples, which the Aztecs prized.

This painting is from a rare Aztec book. It shows Tezcatlipoca, a god the Aztecs adopted from the earlier Toltec culture.

Ancient offerings

In 1978, during excavations for a new underground station, workers stumbled across the remains of the Great Temple of the Aztecs. It was part of a vast religious compound at the heart of Tenochtitlan. Finds from the temple confirmed the Aztec's interest in the earlier cultures of the area.

Archaeologists discovered a mask from Teotihuacan, which was already 800 years old when the Aztecs buried it as an offering. An Olmec mask found buried nearby was a staggering 2,500 years old at the time of the Aztecs. Archaeologists think the Aztecs must have prized these antiques, to offer them up to their gods.

Internet links

For links to websites where you can explore Teotihuacan and visit the Great Temple Museum, go to **www.usborne-quicklinks.com**

South America

South America is rich in natural resources, including precious metals and stones and over 700 varieties of potatoes. Thousands of years ago, its people created stone-built cities and intricate gold and silver ornaments, though wheels and writing were unknown. Europeans arrived in the 16th century, introducing their way of life and destroying whole civilizations. But archaeology is gradually revealing more about earlier cultures.

The Inca inheritance

When the Spanish arrived in South America, the area now called Peru was controlled by the sophisticated empire of the Incas. But archaeology shows the Incas learned their skills from earlier cultures. Tiwanaku was a great religious site and capital from around 500 to 1000. The remains of its sturdy temples show that stone architecture was established long before the Incas. The Chimu empire was based in the city of Chan Chan from around 800 until 1476, when it was conquered by the Incas. But Chimu metalworking skills impressed the Incas so much, they invited the most skilled of the Chimu smiths back to their capital city, to work for them.

This is a Chimu knife, made of gold and turquoise. Several similar knives with curved blades have been found - they may have been used for sacrifices.

The first Americans?

In 1975, a Chilean student of agriculture found some unusually large animal bones at a site at Monte Verde. He took them to his professor, who alerted archaeologists at his university. Excavations revealed the remains of huts made of wood and animal skins, containing clay pits for cooking fires. Simple stone tools were also found, along with bones belonging to mastodons, an ancient relative of the elephant. The Monte Verde mastodon-hunters probably lived around 15,000 years ago. This site is the best preserved example from such an early period in all the Americas.

In the Nazca desert, vast bird and animal designs have been drawn on the ground; see pages 60-61.

The Moche buried their leaders in huge mud pyramids; see pages 56-57.

Many legends have evolved about Machu Picchu and the Incas; see pages 58-59.

Map labels
VENEZUELA
Lake Guatavita
COLOMBIA
ECUADOR
PERU
Dos Cabezas
Sipan
Chan Chan
Chavin de Huantar
Nazca
Machu Picchu
Llanos de Mojos
Lake Titicaca
Tiwanaku
BOLIVIA
CHILE
ARGENTINA
Monte Verde

Internet links

For links to websites where you find out more about raised fields and the gold of El Dorado, go to **www.usborne-quicklinks.com**

El Dorado

When Spanish explorers reached the area which is now Colombia, they became obsessed by a mysterious ceremony which, locals told them, had been enacted on Lake Guatavita in ancient times. A great ruler, painted with gold dust, rowed out onto the lake and scattered gold into the waters. This story grew into the legend of El Dorado, or the Gilded Man, and attracted countless treasure hunters to the lake. But there was no evidence to back up the story. Then, in 1969, a pottery vessel was found in a cave nearby. It contained a gold model of a raft supporting gold figures. The model was made by the Muisca people, who lived in the area from around the 7th century. It may represent the original ceremony at the lake.

This gold raft, made by the Muisca people, was found in 1969. Archaeologists found a similar one in 1856, but it was lost in World War II.

BRAZIL

Chavin culture

The excavation of a site at Chavin de Huantar was the life's work of Peruvian archaeologist Julio Tello. In the 1920s and 30s, he uncovered a great temple, built around a huge stone carved in the shape of a beast, with a cat-like mouth and snaky hair. Objects in a similar style, dating from around 1200 to 200BC, have been found throughout Peru. It seems Chavin de Huantar was an early religious site. Its culture, known as Chavin, spread throughout the Andes region.

Ancient farming

In the 1960s, a visiting geographer was fascinated by straight lines and mounds in the jungle at Llanos de Mojos in Bolivia. They turned out to be part of a system of earthworks, some begun up to 3,000 years ago. Raised fields, with water channels alongside, had been built to grow land and water-loving plants. Larger mounds kept houses safe from the floods which regularly sweep the area. Since these discoveries, raised field farming has been revived around Lake Titicaca in Bolivia and Peru. It protects the local crops from frost damage and nourishes them much better than modern methods.

These peaks are part of the Andes, a huge range of mountains stretching down the west edge of South America. None of the great native civilizations crossed over to the western side.

Royal tombs of the Moche

The Moche people lived on the coast of the country now called Peru, between the 1st and 8th centuries. They buried their dead with impressive goods, often made of solid gold and silver. But, thanks to grave robbers, archaeologists had never managed to find a rich tomb still intact.

This Moche pot was found during a dig at Dos Cabezas. Details from pots like this have provided archaeologists with most of their evidence about the Moche people.

Looters' loss

This all changed, one night in 1987. Police discovered looters at work on a Moche mud-brick pyramid at a place called Sipán. The robbers were probably hoping to find Moche pots, but had stumbled across a tomb packed with gold and silver. Although the site was badly disturbed, archaeologists salvaged what they could, to protect it from further raids. They identified several Moche burials in the pyramid, from different periods.

The main tomb dated from around 290. A wooden coffin contained the skeleton of a man, adorned with massive, but mysterious, gold and silver ornaments. Around him lay the bodies of two women, two men and a dog. Farther down, another important man was buried with gold beads decorated with spiders' webs. Archaeologists had never found anything like this before. But other Moche artifacts gave them hints as to how the precious ornaments had been worn.

These snarling heads portrayed on a Moche pot match copper beads found at Sipán.

This Moche pyramid, near Trujillo in Peru, is made of mud brick. It has been worn down by rainstorms and looters to one third its original size.

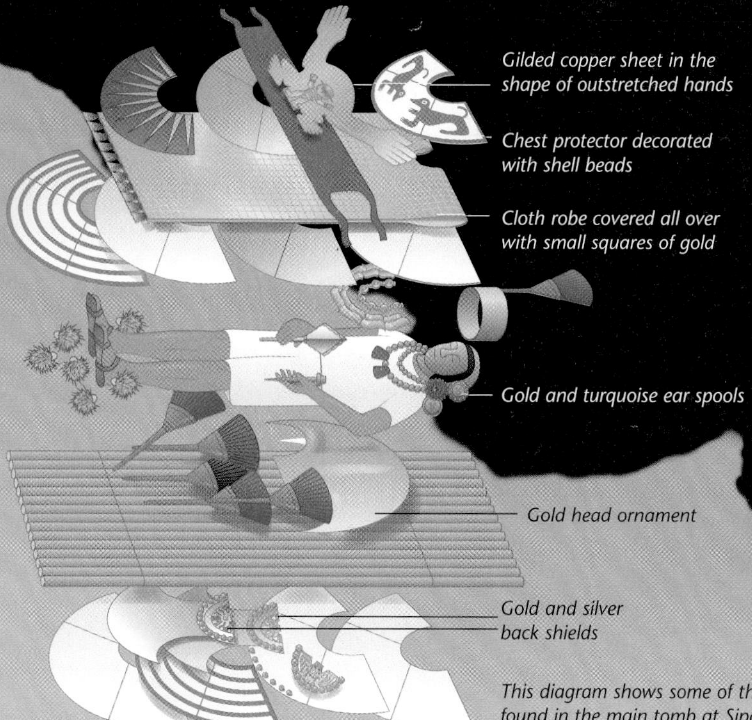

Gilded copper sheet in the shape of outstretched hands

Chest protector decorated with shell beads

Cloth robe covered all over with small squares of gold

Gold and turquoise ear spools

Gold head ornament

Gold and silver back shields

This diagram shows some of the goods found in the main tomb at Sipán. The layers have been spread out to give a clearer view.

Stolen goods

In 1997-1999, a team located and excavated three more undisturbed tombs in the pyramid at a site named Dos Cabezas. More metal ornaments were found, alongside pots with details similar to several items from the Sipán tombs. These discoveries have given archaeologists more clues about the Moche than ever before.

Looting is an ongoing problem, at many archaeological sites around the world. It is funded by wealthy international collectors who pay high prices for historic artifacts but don't care how they are obtained. This black market wrecks archaeological sites, as crucial finds, including human remains, are plundered in the search for gold and jewels.

Clues in the clay

Many Moche pots are in the shape of people, with detailed clothing and ornaments. Others are decorated with drawings showing every aspect of Moche life, from childbirth to bread-making. This was a great help in identifying the more mysterious ornaments found in the tomb at Sipán.

Some of the large, gold and silver objects from the tomb are just like the nose ornaments and headdresses shown on pots being worn by priestly figures; others match the shields warrior figures are shown wearing to protect their backs. This suggests the men buried at Sipán were warriors and priests. They must have been very important to be buried inside the pyramid, which was the site of Moche religious ceremonies.

This gold and turquoise ear ornament was found in the main burial at Sipán. The central figure is dressed very like the body found with it.

Weaving a legend

In 1534, Spanish conquerors took control of the area now called Peru. They found a vast empire, with paved roads and stone-built cities, led by a ruler known as the Inca. But the Spanish treated the Inca people as slaves, and destroyed their culture and way of life. Archaeologists are now trying to piece together the evidence, to find out more about the lost civilization of the Incas.

Machu Pichu is perched on a high and remote mountainside. Legends say it was the last refuge of the Incas against the Spanish, but archaeologists now think it was a royal villa, not a fortress.

Main temple

Gateway to the complex

Royal palace

The stone buildings had pointed thatched roofs which have since decayed.

Fit for the Inca

When US explorer Hiram Bingham located Machu Pichu in 1911, he became convinced he had found the legendary "lost city of the Incas", the fortress where they held out, after the Spanish invasion. But Machu Pichu is covered in the remains of fine, stone-built temples, baths and luxurious apartments. It's now clear it was a luxury royal retreat and religious site, rather than a city or fortress. The real Inca fortress of Vilacamba has now been located several valleys away.

Sometimes, legends can get in the way of archaeology. This is especially true of the Inca civilization. Although they had an advanced culture, the Incas never developed writing, so the only written records that survive were made by the Spanish invaders. As they didn't understand or care about the Incas, their reports were often wildly inaccurate.

Internet links

For a link to a website where you can unwrap the fabric bundles around an Inca mummy and find the artifacts hidden inside, go to **www.usborne-quicklinks.com**

Tangled tales

But even though they didn't have writing, the Incas did leave behind some records. They kept their accounts using a system of knots, tied on dyed strings of cotton or llama wool. These tallies are known as *khipu*. Only a few hundred have survived, but archaeologists can now "read" the knots of many of them, revealing how the Incas managed their goods and supplies.

Some khipu have remained undecipherable. It is possible that the knots on these represent words which make up stories or histories. If this knotty problem is solved, it may reveal a great deal more about the way the Incas viewed and recorded their world.

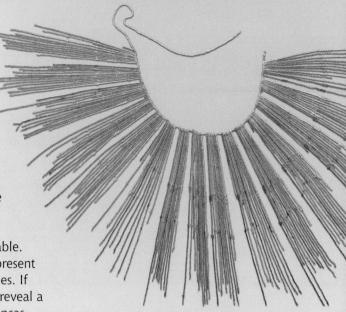

This is a number khipu. Different numbers are indicated by different types of knots and their position on the various strings.

Living quarters and workshops

Women weavers

Archaeologists also think the Incas may have recorded stories and information in the fabrics they wove. Even Spanish writers noted the distinct patterns and fabrics worn by different ranks of Inca society. They also reported that the best cloth, woven by special women called *aklla*, was reserved for the Inca himself.

Because of this, archaeologists are especially interested in small female figures found in many Inca graves and shrines. They may represent aklla weavers, and their tiny cloaks give a tantalizing glimpse of the kind of cloth the Inca himself may have worn.

Feather headdress

Gold female figure

Miniature robes of finely woven cloth

Many statuettes like these have been found in Inca burials and mountaintop shrines. They may be meant to represent the women who wove cloth for the Inca.

Lines in the desert

In the stony, windswept desert at Nazca in Peru, thousands of lines are marked out on the ground. Some run straight across the vast landscape for miles, while others mark out the shapes of animals, plants and other patterns hundreds of feet long. These designs were made more than a thousand years ago, but they can only be appreciated from the air. From the ground they are too huge to see. So who made them, and why?

Alien landing?

In the mid 20th century, when people first saw the number and scale of the Nazca lines from the windows of a plane, they were amazed. Little was known then about the people who had lived in the area at the time the lines were made, and all sorts of crazy theories sprang up. Some people even suggested the lines were created as landing strips for alien spacecraft.

But careful study of the area and its archaeology has shown that the lines were made by quite ordinary people. Large amounts of pottery have been found near some of the animal designs, and this matches up with pottery and textiles found in the graves of people buried nearby around 2,000 years ago. The animal and bird designs on the pots are very similar to the line designs, so it's clear they were made by the same, local people.

This aerial photograph shows one of the animal designs at Nazca - a vast drawing of a hummingbird with a wingspan of over 90m (300 ft).

This Nazca pot is decorated with hummingbirds, similar to the huge design drawn in the desert. You can see this especially in the wing feathers and the feet.

Internet links

For a link to a website where you can see pictures and 3-D virtual models of the Nazca lines, go to **www.usborne-quicklinks.com**

Drawing the line

The desert at Nazca has a stony surface, which is dark brown from the scouring effect of the harsh winds in the region. But if the stones are moved, the pale sand underneath shows up against the darker background. Modern archaeologists have shown exactly how this could have been done to produce the lines.

These diagrams show how modern archeologists made their own lines in the Nazca desert. First they lined up poles with a point on the horizon.

Then they just cleared away the stones directly under the string guide line and piled them up at the edges of the cleared strip.

Laying out curves and detailed patterns would have been more complex, but it would still have been possible using just a few poles and some string. To make the animal designs, archaeologists think the ancient Nazca people probably just scaled up measurements taken from a design on one of their pots. So it's no longer a mystery how the lines were created. But archaeologists are still trying to discover why these huge designs might have been made.

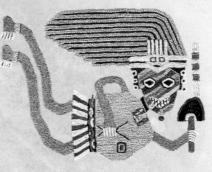

These are flying gods depicted on textiles from around 1000-500BC, found at Paracas, near Nazca. Archaeological evidence suggests the Nazca people believed in sky gods like these.

Sky gods

The latest research about the religious beliefs of the Nazca people suggests sky gods played an important role. People living in the area today can still point out bird and animal shapes in the stars above the desert.

It seems likely that the lines and patterns were laid out as part of the Nazca people's religious beliefs. They may have drawn the huge designs, which can't be seen by people on the ground, for their gods to see. There's also evidence that they used some of the lines as pathways, and this may have been part of a religious ritual too.

Australasia and Oceania

The area known as Australasia is made up of Australia, New Zealand and Papua New Guinea. Oceania is a collection of over 20,000 islands stretching out into the Pacific Ocean. The land mass of Australia is so vast it's counted as a continent on its own, but it is not surprising that a lot of the area's archaeology and history is to do with the sea.

PACIFIC OCEAN

Kuk Swamp

PAPUA NEW GUINEA

SOLOMON ISLANDS

VANUATU

FIJI

Kakadu

Kakadu National Park is a rich site for Aboriginal rock art; see pages 64-65.

NEW CALEDONIA

Lapita

AUSTRALIA

Whangape Harbour

NEW ZEALAND

Port Arthur

Maori carvings

In 2002, divers discovered a blade made of greenstone on the sea bed at Whangape Harbour, at the northern tip of New Zealand. This was a rare find. Blades like these were made for ceremonial wood-shaping tools – known as adzes – by the Maoris, a people who settled in New Zealand sometime in the 12th century. The greenstone was traded amongst Maori settlers as a precious stone, and became an important part of the Maori way of life. Greenstone adzes were very difficult to make, so their owners treasured them. It's unusual for an archaeologist to find one.

This is a Maori greenstone carving of a sea monster. It dates from the 18th century, and was worn as a pendant.

Port Arthur

On an isolated neck of land on the island of Tasmania, south of the Australian mainland, stand the ruins of Port Arthur prison settlement. In 1833, the British authorities began shipping convicted criminals to the site, where they worked in terrible conditions to build ships. When the transportation of convicts ended in 1852, prisons like Port Arthur gradually fell into decay and their history was forgotten. But archaeologists are now excavating the remains of buildings and gardens at Port Arthur. One recent find is a sunken saw-pit, where convicts cut up timber.

Lapita pottery

In 1952, excavations in New Caledonia uncovered some unusual fragments of pottery, marked with intricate stamped decorations. Radiocarbon dating revealed the pottery was from as far back as 800BC. Archaeologists named the style of pottery after the place it was first discovered - a site which local people called "Lapita". Since then, even older Lapita pottery, dating from around 3,500 to 2,000 years ago, has been found at sites from New Guinea to Samoa. The people who made the pottery must have been expert seafarers to spread the style over such vast stretches of the Pacific Ocean. Some pieces of Lapita pottery, like this one, are decorated with faces, giving archaeologists a glimpse of the people who made them.

SAMOA

This fragment of Lapita pottery dates from about 1000BC. It was found on the Solomon Islands.

Prehistoric gardens

Aerial photographs taken in 1972 revealed a regular grid pattern on the landscape at Kuk Swamp, in the highlands of New Guinea. It was made by the remains of a very ancient system of drainage ditches and gardens. These were used to grow food plants, including taro, a root vegetable still farmed in the area, and yams and bananas. Excavation also revealed several layers of ash from a nearby volcano. These were dated by comparing them with other ash deposits in the area. Along with radiocarbon dates from other materials found at the site, this evidence showed that people were growing crops at Kuk Swamp as early as 7,000BC.

Internet links

For links to websites where you can read more about Lapita pottery and Port Arthur prison, go to **www.usborne-quicklinks.com**

Voyage of discovery

There are many theories about how the people of the Pacific islands got there, and where they originally came from. It's now generally agreed that they set off from New Guinea in canoes and gradually worked their way east across the Pacific Ocean, even reaching Easter Island, around 7,000km (4,000 miles) east of New Zealand, by the year 700. To find out how they managed it, archaeologists have built and sailed replica boats made to ancient designs. Only fragments of ancient canoes have been found. So archaeologists have to rely on a few early drawings and clues from traditional canoes, which are still being built and used in the Pacific region today. Ancient canoes built for long ocean voyages would have been much bigger than the one shown here, but the basic design would have been similar.

This sailing canoe, from the Cook Islands to the east of Fiji, is built to a traditional design that probably dates back thousands of years.

The changing land

The aboriginal people of Australia lived there for thousands of years before the first European settlers arrived. Aboriginal art, legends and traditional ways of life have left archaeologists many clues about how people, plants and animals gradually adapted to each other, over the years.

Sign of the times

Kakadu in northwest Australia contains some of Australia's most interesting rock paintings and carvings. There are all sorts of styles, and it is known that local aboriginal people were adding their own paintings until the 1970s. It can be hard to tell which ones are early and which ones are more recent, but archaeologists have developed several methods of dating rock art. Some involve radioactive tests, but others are based on the style and subjects of the art.

Aboriginal legends have been painted in similar ways for thousands of years, but sometimes something new is shown. This can also give clues about the date of the art. One rock painting at Kakadu shows a European sailing ship. This type of ship only reached Australia in 1642, so the painting must have been made after this date.

These figures on a rock at Kakadu are drawn in the traditional "X-ray" style of aboriginal painting, but the modern blue pigment shows they were made recently.

Internet links

For a link to a website with more rock art from Kakadu, go to **www.usborne-quicklinks.com**

Playing the dating game

The materials used in rock paintings can also hold clues to their age. Aboriginal artists sometimes used organic materials, such as wax, in their paints. Archaeologists can obtain rough dates for these paints by radiocarbon dating. Modern pigments can be dated even more accurately. The figures in the painting above are decorated with a distinctive blue pigment. Aboriginal artists got this from a domestic laundry dye, used from around 1900.

Recently, archaeologists have been investigating rock varnish, as a means of dating rock art. Rock varnish is a thin layer of windblown particles that builds up on exposed rocks. Among the particles are some tiny parts of plants, and these can be dated by radiocarbon dating. Archaeologists know that any rock varnish they find on top of rock art was blown on to the rock after the painting was made. So the rock art must be earlier than the date of the varnish.

Rising waters

The style of rock paintings can also help archaeologists date the art, but it can give important clues about changes in the environment, too. Rock art styles at Kakadu have helped archaeologists find out how rises in sea levels several thousand years ago affected this area of Australia.

One style of rock art at Kakadu shows large, realistic pictures of land animals, such as kangaroos. A later style of art, known as "X-ray", shows marine animals, such as saltwater crocodiles and Barramundi fish, which are usually found at the coast. Archaeologists think the art style changed around 7,000 years ago, when sea levels rose, driving away land animals and bringing new, marine creatures to the area. So the art gives important clues as to which animals were affected as the sea reached farther inland.

This is painting of a kangaroo at Kakadu is in the style used before the rise in sea levels. It may be up to 20,000 years old.

Changing the land

Other types of archaeological evidence also record changes in Australia's ancient environment. Ancient pollen and charcoal particles, trapped in sediment at the bottom of lakes, show that in the distant past there was a dramatic change in Australia's natural environment. At some point many thousands of years ago, there was a huge increase in Eucalyptus trees and a decline in many other, more delicate plant species.

Traditional aboriginal methods of controlled burning, shown here, are being revived. They prevent huge bushfires by burning off dry debris.

It's possible this change was caused by the aboriginal people learning how to use controlled fires in the Australian bushland. Some aboriginal people still use fires to drive animals into traps and to stimulate plants to produce edible shoots. This method, known as fire-stick farming, leads to an increase in plants that survive repeated burning, such as Eucalyptus trees, but kills off other varieties. This matches the change recorded in the archaeological evidence but it is not clear when it took place. Some archaeologists think it happened naturally, as early as 128,000 years ago - before humans arrived in Australia. Others think it was caused by people arriving around 60,000 years ago.

Easter Island statues

On a tiny, treeless island, surrounded by the Pacific Ocean for thousands of miles in every direction, stand hundreds of huge stone statues. Archaeologists have wondered for many years how they got there, and what they were for. But the mysterious statues also hold the secret of a forgotten environmental disaster.

A map of Easter Island, showing important archaeological sites.

Anakena

Rano Raraku quarry

Hanga Roa

Ancient mystery

The ancestors of the modern Easter Islanders carved and transported the huge statues, known as *moai*, to villages all around the island. When Europeans first visited Easter Island in 1722, they couldn't understand how the local people had created such impressive monuments with the simple tools they had. But modern experiments have shown how they did it.

It's now known that nearly all the statues were carved at one quarry, at Rano Raraku. Its soft volcanic rock was carved using hammer stones made of harder rock, also found on the island. Hundreds of unfinished moai are still attached to the quarry, partly carved. This helps show how they were made.

This archaeologist is marking up a moai for a computer survey. The soft rock of the statues is wearing away, but the computer record will preserve their details for years to come.

Chipping away

The unfinished moai are flat on their backs. Carvers started at the top and worked around the sides. Then they wedged stones under the statue to keep it steady, while they chipped away underneath: a dangerous operation. They probably used wooden sleds or rollers to drag the statues into position.

Carvers also made eyes to fit into the statues' eye sockets, although it's thought these were only put in place for special ceremonies. All the statues also had heavy topknots, or *pukao*, made of a different, reddish stone, placed on top of their heads.

This diagram shows how the topknots might have been raised.

1. Push down on lever.
2. Topknot is pulled up.
3. Apply brake.
4. Repeat until topknot reaches the top.

Raising the topknot stones was quite a feat, as they are extremely heavy. There are many theories about how it was done, but a frame of wood and ropes, like the one in the diagram, could be operated easily by just a few people.

Internet links

For a link to a website where you can play a game to help move a moai, go to **www.usborne-quicklinks.com**

These moai stand on an ahu, or ceremonial platform. They were knocked over by a tidal wave in 1960, but have been put back.

This is the eye from a moai, found at Anakena on Easter Island. It is made of red stone surrounded by white coral.

Triumph and disaster

With these simple techniques and tools, the islanders created amazing and impressive monuments. But they also used up too many of the island's natural resources. Statue-building came to a sudden end around 1680. Archaeological pollen records show that the palm trees which used to grow on Easter Island died out at around this time.

The islanders themselves were partly to blame, as they had cut down too many trees to move their statues. They had to pay the price for stripping the island of its trees. The islanders probably came to Easter Island in traditional wooden canoes, but when the trees died out, they became stranded. They had to endure troubled times of war and disease as they competed with each other for the island's dwindling resources.

The topknot has been put back on this moai.

Asia

Asia is an enormous and varied continent, encompassing vast deserts and the highest mountains and lowest valleys in the world. Some of the oldest and most spectacular civilizations have developed there, providing a rich source of archaeological remains.

The first cities

Since the mid-19th century, archaeologists have been excavating sites in the fertile lands between the mighty Tigris and Euphrates rivers in the Middle East. Historians call this region Mesopotamia, which means "the land between the rivers" in Greek. It was here that the world's earliest civilizations developed and where the first cities such as Ur and Eridu grew up from around 4000BC. In 1964, archaeologists at Ebla in Syria discovered a library of 20,000 clay tablets inscribed with the earliest form of writing called cuneiform.

TURKEY
Excavations have found evidence of cities mentioned in the Bible; see pages 70-71.

Ebla · Nimrud
Jericho · SYRIA
JORDAN
Petra · Babylon
IRAQ · Ur · Behistun
Eridu · Persepolis

KAZAKHSTAN

UZBEKISTAN

IRAN

AFGHANISTAN

SAUDI ARABIA

Harappa

PAKISTAN
Mohenjo-Daro

OMAN

YEMEN

To find out more about Harappa and Mohenjo-Daro, cities of the Harappan civilization; see pages 72-73.

INDIA

Internet links

For links to websites where you can see more artifacts from Asia, go to **www.usborne-quicklinks.com**

Great empires

The ruins of Persepolis lie in the fertile plains of Iran. Huge carvings on the buildings have told archaeologists much about the history of the Persian empire. At Behistun, archaeologists translated ancient Persian inscriptions, which later helped them to decipher an even older language called Akkadian.

Carving of King Darius, who founded Persepolis in 518BC.

Trade riches

One of the most famous archaeological sites of all is the ancient city of Petra in Jordan. It has been excavated over the past 100 years, but the remains of the city cover such a vast area that much of it still lies buried under the sand. Petra was carved from the rocks more than 2,000 years ago by people called the Nabataeans, who made it the capital of their vast trading empire.

The great trade routes of the world criss-crossed the mountains, deserts and plains of Asia for thousands of years. Cities and empires rose and fell with this trade, growing rich from the silks, spices and other rare goods that were carried across their borders.

Royal tombs

The earliest known Chinese civilization, called the Shang, developed in the Huang He valley from about 1800BC. The city of Anyang was the Shang capital from the 14th until the 11th centuries BC and contains the tombs of the last Shang rulers. The tombs were robbed in ancient times. But the few surviving remains excavated from the 1920s, including bronze sculptures, give an idea of the objects that must have been inside.

Archaeologists found superb bronze objects in the Anyang tombs, like this head of a god.

Buried in the jungle

In Cambodia lie the magnificent ruins of Angkor, capital of the Khmers from the 11th to 14th centuries. For centuries the city lay lost in a thick jungle. At the end of the 19th century, the jungle around the ruins was cut down, revealing the beautiful carved stone buildings once again. Recent radar images have shown that much more still lies buried at Angkor including six more temples, as yet unexcavated.

This is part of the temple of Angkor Wat at Angkor, covered in enormous carvings.

RUSSIA

Frozen remains of Steppe Nomad leaders and their rich furnishings have been found in tombs at this site; see page 19.

— **Pazyryk**

MONGOLIA

JAPAN

● **Shirakawa-go**

CHINA

● *Anyang*

● *Li Shan*

Traditional farm houses survive in this part of Japan; see pages 76-77.

Hundreds of baked clay warriors, buried with an emperor, were found here; see pages 74-75.

BURMA (MYANMAR)   VIETNAM

THAILAND

Angkor ●

CAMBODIA

PHILIPPINES

MALAYSIA

INDONESIA

Steppe nomads

The Steppes is the name given to a huge swathe of grassland stretching from the edge of Europe to China. For thousands of years the region was inhabited by nomadic people. They left few traces, except for their burial mounds. Since the early 20th century, archaeologists in Siberia have been excavating these mounds, and have uncovered leather, fabric and preserved bodies, dating to around 450BC.

The Bible lands

During the 19th century, some archaeologists set out to find the sites mentioned in the Bible and developed an area of research known as biblical archaeology. Their work, and that of other archaeologists excavating in the region, proved that many of the sites really did exist. But some turned out to be much older than they had expected.

Did the walls of Jericho fall down?

Yes, and no. In the Bible, it is written that Joshua and the Hebrews surrounded the town of Jericho, in present-day Palestine, and the walls came crashing down. During excavations led by Kathleen Kenyon in the 1950s, archaeologists proved that the town had existed in biblical times and that it did have a high wall around it. But they discovered that the earliest wall was probably meant to protect Jericho from floods, rather than invasion. They also found that Jericho was one of the oldest towns in the world, dating back to at least 8000BC. This is about 7,000 years before the time it is mentioned in the Bible.

Warriors of the Bible

Some of the most remarkable biblical discoveries have been made among the ruins of Nimrud in present-day Iraq. From 883BC until 710BC, Nimrud had been the capital city of the Assyrians, who are described as ferocious warriors in the Bible.

Austen Layard found this sculpture of King Ashurnasirpal II (who reigned from 883-859BC) in the ruins of a temple at Nimrud.

At Nimrud, in 1845-47, a scholar named Austen Layard uncovered the remains of vast palaces and royal halls. Their huge stone walls were covered in sculptures of Assyrian kings, soldiers and their prisoners. These discoveries made a great impact, as it was the first time that the names of some of the people, places and events described in the Bible had been found in inscriptions. Some of the sculptures even depicted the people themselves.

A royal cemetery

One of the first cities mentioned in the Bible is Ur, which dates from around 3000BC. It was one of the main sites of the Sumerian civilization, one of the earliest in the world, which developed in the southern part of present-day Iraq.

This golden necklace is just one of the objects Leonard Woolley found in the royal graves at Ur.

During the 1920s, an archaeologist called Leonard Woolley carried out detailed excavations at Ur. He found the remains of mud brick houses and a huge stepped temple called a ziggurat. Woolley also made a more spectacular, though horrifying, discovery. He found the graves of the early kings and queens of Ur which also contained the bodies of dozens of guards and royal servants. Woolley believed that they had all poisoned themselves, so that they could remain with their masters and serve them forever. He also found fabulous gold and silver artifacts buried with the bodies in the royal graves.

This land, beside the River Euphrates on the borders of Syria and Iraq, was where some of the earliest civilizations in the world developed. Many archaeological discoveries have been made here.

The city of legends

Babylon is one of the most infamous cities in the Bible, but to the ancient Greeks its hanging gardens were one of the Seven Wonders of the World. In 1899, a German archaeologist named Robert Koldewey began excavating the site. Over the next 18 years, he and his team uncovered a huge area of the city and made some amazing discoveries, including the ruins of the Ishtar Gate, a brilliant blue ceremonial gateway. They also found the remains of a high wall with arches, which they believed was the site of the Hanging Gardens. But archaeologists today think they are in fact part of the palace of King Nebuchadnezzar. Recent excavations on the banks of the Euphrates river have uncovered massive terraces, which may be the true site of the gardens.

This modern reconstruction, based on surviving tile and brick fragments, shows what the Ishtar Gate may have looked like.

Internet links

For a link to a website where you can discover more about all these different sites and cultures, play games and try out activities, go to
www.usborne-quicklinks.com

Cities of the Indus Valley

The site of Harappa on the River Indus in Pakistan was first discovered in the 19th century. But at that time no one knew just how old it was. Then, in the 1920s, archaeologist John Marshall excavated it and another site nearby called Mohenjo-Daro. He was amazed to discover that the remains of these two cities dated to 2500BC, much earlier than anything known in the region before.

Harappan civilization

The two cities were part of a great civilization which archaeologists have named the Harappan or Indus Valley civilization. Since these cities were first excavated, the remains of many more towns and villages have been found dotted about the Indus Valley. But archaeologists have found more extensive remains at Mohenjo-Daro and so this site has provided them with the most information about the Harappan civilization.

The wide, fertile plains of the Indus river in Pakistan, shown here, are the site of some of the earliest and most important archaeological discoveries in the Indian subcontinent.

The excavations at Harappa unearthed wonderful sculptures, including this pottery figurine of a mother goddess.

Internet links

For a link to a website where you can explore the ancient city of Mohenjo-Daro, go to **www.usborne-quicklinks.com**

The heart of government

Excavations at Mohenjo-Daro have shown that it was an extremely well-planned city. The upper part of the city, known as the citadel, contained all the important public buildings. They were built of baked brick and included a huge colonnaded hall, rooms that were possibly used by officials, and a bathhouse which may have been used for washing before religious ceremonies.

This reconstruction of the Mohenjo-Daro bathhouse is based on archaeological finds.

The roof was made of planks and beaten earth. It rested on strong, wooden poles.

Some of the side rooms contained bathtubs.

The main walls were very thick and were made of bricks plastered with mud.

The central bathing area was 12m (40ft) long and 7m (23ft) wide.

The huge drain was more than 2m (6ft) high, and ran underground. It had a cover over it that could be lifted for inspection.

This is a soapstone statue of an important Harappan official or god. Archaeologists are unsure who the rulers of the Harappan civilization were. Some believe that the cities may have been ruled by a council of officials rather than a single person.

A mysterious end

The reasons why the civilization came to an end are still mysterious. It started to decline from about 1800BC, but there is no sign of an invasion or of a disaster such as an earthquake. The people may have ruined their farmland by growing too many crops and cutting down too many trees. But while cities like Harappa and Mohenjo-Daro slowly declined and were eventually abandoned, smaller settlements in adjacent areas began to flourish.

Modern dangers

Today, Mohenjo-Daro faces new dangers. The water table is rising, bringing corrosive salts which are destroying the foundations of the buildings. The result is that they may soon collapse and dissolve back into the ground.

The best water around

The people enjoyed some of the best water and sanitation facilities in the ancient world, with bathrooms and lavatories in many houses. An elaborate drainage system ran under the streets, with inspection holes placed at regular intervals. Most people - as many as 40,000 - lived and worked in the lower part of the city, below the citadel. Wide streets were laid out on a grid pattern and lined with square, mud brick houses.

The march of death

In 1974 some farmers digging a well in eastern China made an extraordinary discovery: they found a life-size model of an ancient Chinese soldier. Archaeologists had already been working in the area for many years, but when they started excavating this new site they were amazed at what they saw. They eventually uncovered more than 7,000 soldiers, buried for over 2,000 years. Excavations have been continuing ever since and have revealed many other wonderful discoveries, including a team of bronze horses pulling a bronze chariot.

This portrait of Qin Shi Huangdi, whose tomb the terracotta soldiers were meant to protect, was painted many centuries after his death.

The terracotta army

The soldiers were made from a type of clay called terracotta and had been buried near the tomb of the first emperor of China. He was called Qin Shi Huangdi and he ruled from about 221 until 210BC. Earlier Chinese rulers, such as the Shang kings, had been buried with real soldiers and members of their court, who were sacrificed for the occasion. Archaeologists had already found the tombs of later rulers and nobles buried with small clay figures of people instead of real humans. Many hundreds of these had been found. But they never dreamed that they would find any figures as large as this, let alone an entire army of them.

The life-size soldiers were found all lined up in battle formation. Their different uniforms, weapons and hairstyles indicate their rank.

More surprises

The archaeologists spent three years excavating the first burial chamber alone. News of their discoveries quickly spread around the world, and so many people came to have a look at the site that a new road and even an airport had to be built. During this construction work, the builders and archaeologists found further chambers containing even more soldiers.

Internet links

For a link to a website where you can see more pictures of the terracotta soldiers, go to **www.usborne-quicklinks.com**

Ready for battle

So far, archaeologists have excavated three vast underground chambers. They found Qin Shi Huangdi's soldiers in various positions. Some are clearly archers, kneeling to shoot their arrows, some are foot soldiers, and others are charioteers. They all look poised to go into battle for their emperor.

This diagram shows the layout of the burial pits. There were three main pits, each lined with timbers. Pit 2 is shown here in detail.

The burial area covers 25,000 sq m (30,000 sq yds).

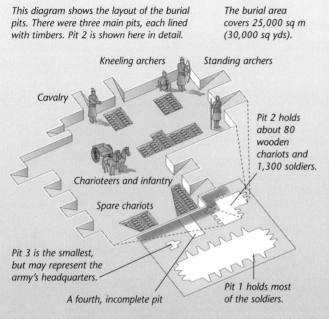

Kneeling archers

Standing archers

Cavalry

Pit 2 holds about 80 wooden chariots and 1,300 soldiers.

Charioteers and infantry

Spare chariots

Pit 3 is the smallest, but may represent the army's headquarters.

A fourth, incomplete pit

Pit 1 holds most of the soldiers.

Mystery mausoleum

The terracotta soldiers' burial chambers are just one part of an enormous underground city complex built of stone and covering an area of about 10.5 sq km (4 sq miles). When he died, Qin Shi Huangdi himself was buried in a huge mausoleum at the heart of the city. This lies beneath a giant mound and there are plans to excavate it. There are stories that the royal burial chamber is protected by crossbows, set to fire automatically at anyone who tries to enter.

Different faces

What's remarkable about these soldiers is that they all seem to have different faces, even though they were not sculpted individually. The archaeologists have noticed that there are several different styles of eyes, ears, noses and other features. These were probably made in batches and different combinations applied to the figures, to give each one an individual appearance.

The statues were originally brightly painted and some of the paint still survives. Conservators have discovered that many of the figures are now deteriorating from the humidity caused by the breath of tourists. In the future they may have to restrict the number of visitors to the site.

In this close-up of one of the soldiers, you can see the face, hair and body protection in incredible detail.

Japanese minka

For thousands of years, farmers in rural Japan used natural materials such as wood and grasses to build their own houses, known as *minka*. In the aftermath of World War II, massive changes swept Japan, bringing Western construction methods that gradually replaced the minka. So archaeologists have stepped in to record and preserve the few remaining examples.

This map shows some of Japan's most important minka sites.

Living space

There are several traditional designs of minka, with roof shapes to suit the particular weather conditions in different regions of Japan. All these designs have been around since at least the 6th century. Archaeologists know this from small clay models of different minka types, found in graves from this period. But the buildings themselves also preserve evidence of the ways the interior layout has developed.

Studies of standing minka, and excavations of sites where minka once stood, have also given archaeologists plenty of information about how the buildings developed on the inside. Some arrangements evolved to suit particular climates, but others seem to have been more to do with customs and traditions.

This clay model of a farmhouse, or minka, was found in a 6th-century Japanese tomb. Its roof is a very steeply-angled version of the irimoya roof, shown to the right.

A kirizuma roof

A yosemune roof

An irimoya roof

Floor plan

Archaeological evidence shows that very early minka had just two rooms: a raised *kamite*, used for eating and sleeping, and an earth-floored *doma*, used for cooking and working. Over time, people started separating off more rooms in the kamite, for specific leisure activities, but the doma remained as a multi-purpose working area. Archaeologists have found several customs, still followed in present-day minka, that help explain why the two areas developed differently.

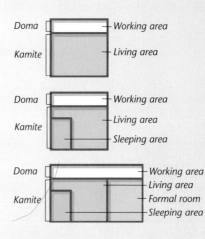

These plans show how the floor plan may have developed in some minka farmhouses.

Even today, everyone has to remove their shoes before they enter the kamite. Some rooms in the kamite are only used on special occasions, and there are also fixed places for the master and mistress of the house, and for guests, in the dining area. The same rules don't apply in the doma. These customs show archaeologists that the doma has come to be seen as the informal part of the house, while the kamite is regarded as formal, even though people go there after the day's work, to relax.

These traditional Japanese farm buildings are in an open-air musuem in Takayama. The largest is a farmhouse, or minka.

Recycled houses

Archaeologists have also rediscovered something that farmers always knew. Although minka are made of natural materials, they last very well. Farmers built their houses with the things that grew around them, which they could get for free. Local wood provided the framework, with mud plastered on top to keep out rain and wind, and a roof of grasses, reeds or bark. But these natural materials, which made minka so durable and cheap to build, are part of the reason for their decline. It's very difficult and expensive to get hold of them today, and the skills needed to build with them are dying out. Archaeologists hoping to preserve minka buildings, and the way of life that goes with them, have set up projects to help people restore and maintain their minka using traditional methods and materials.

Some minka are also officially protected. In 1995, the villages of Shirakawa-go and Gokayama were registered as World Heritage sites because of their unique minka, the oldest dating from the 17th century.

Internet links

For a link to a website where you see photos of a minka being built, go to **www.usborne-quicklinks.com**

These shoes were left outside by people entering the formal area of a traditional Japanese house. Customs like these can tell archaeologists a lot about how these houses developed.

Europe

Europe is a small continent, but within its borders the landscapes are very diverse - mountains, valleys, plains and lush farmland. The region has given birth to some of the greatest civilizations, leaving behind a rich variety of archaeological remains. Here are just a few of them.

Lady of Elche

One day in August 1897, a 14-year-old boy was helping his parents bring in the harvest from their fields near the southern Spanish town of Elche. He stumbled across a magnificent stone sculpture of a woman half-buried in the ground. She was carved wearing elaborate necklaces and a headdress, and traces of red paint were on her lips and cloak. Dating to 400BC, the sculpture told archaeologists that there was a very sophisticated culture in Spain dating back earlier than anything they had previously known.

This sculpture of the Lady of Elche was carved by the Iberian people of Spain, before the time of the Romans.

SWEDEN

The Vasa, a 17th century warship, was recovered here; see page 20.

NORWAY

FINLAND

Stockholm

ESTONIA

UNITED KINGDOM

An entire Viking street was found preserved at York; see pages 88-89.

DENMARK

Trundholm

LITHUANIA

Newgrange

York

These late Stone Age monuments may have been used to keep track of the sun; see pages 82-83.

Prittlewell

Stonehenge

GERMANY

A Bronze Age astronomical device was found here; see pages 82-83.

Nebra

POLAND

BELARUS

Ice Age mammoth hunters left remains here; see pages 80-81.

Mezhirich

CZECH REPUBLIC

Hochdorf

FRANCE

Carnac

SWITZERLAND

AUSTRIA

Otztaler Alps

Lascaux

ITALY

Frozen remains of a man from 3,300BC were found here; see page 18.

ROMANIA

Altamira

Ice Age paintings of animals adorn the walls of caves at these sites; see pages 80-81.

SPAIN

SERBIA AND MONTENEGRO

Tarquinia
Rome

Elche

Pompeii

GREECE

Ancient Greek remains from Athens still cause debate; see page 84.

Athens

Spectacular Roman remains still stand in the ancient capital of the empire; see page 85.

These towns were preserved by volcanic ash; see pages 86-87.

Akrotiri

A chieftain's grave

A spectacular discovery was made in 1978, when archaeologists excavating a mound at Hochdorf in Germany found the body of a man laid out on a huge bronze bed. Superb gold ornaments had been buried with him. He turned out to be a chief of one of the tribes of the Celtic people, who dominated parts of Europe from about 800BC until AD50. The burial dates to around 550BC and gives us a wonderful picture of life and death in Celtic Europe.

🐴 Sun chariot

This bronze chariot, found at Trundholm, is 60cm (2ft) long and dates back to around 1350BC.

In 1902, a farmer dug up a model of a horse and chariot in his fields near Trundholm in Denmark. Thinking that it was a toy, he gave it to his daughter to play with. But when it was later examined by archaeologists, they found that it was 3,500 years old and a masterpiece of Bronze Age metalworking. The horse is pulling a large golden circle which may represent the sun. Archaeologists think the model may have been buried as a religious offering.

RUSSIA

UKRAINE

📯 The golden chamber

In 2003, archaeologists digging at Prittlewell in southeastern England found a burial chamber full of artifacts dating to around 650, including a gold buckle and glass jars. The quality of the goods indicates that someone very important was buried there, possibly an Anglo-Saxon king. This was the most important Anglo-Saxon discovery since gold and silver grave goods were found at nearby Sutton Hoo in 1939.

One of the glass jars found in the Prittlewell burial

🚶 Seeing inside

The Etruscans ruled an area of Tuscany in Italy between about 900 and 400BC. They buried their dead in underground tombs, the walls decorated with wonderful paintings. Over the centuries, many of these tombs have been looted. In the 1950s, an Italian archaeologist named Carlo Lerici designed a probe with a light and camera on the end. This could be used to see into the tombs to find out which had been looted and which were worth excavating.

This lively scene of musicians was painted in one of the Etruscan tombs.

Internet links

For a link to a website where you can find out more about the Prittlewell burial, go to **www.usborne-quicklinks.com**

The big freeze

This is a reconstruction of an Ice Age house made of mammoth bones. The original was found at Mezhirich in the Ukraine, and is the earliest surviving form of architecture ever discovered.

Around 20,000 years ago, vast ice sheets covered much of Europe and only stunted trees grew. This period of extreme cold is known as the Ice Age. Life was hard for the people of the Ice Age. Archaeologists have uncovered evidence that shows some of the ways they managed to survive. But finds such as cave paintings and sculptures also suggest that art and rituals flourished under these harsh conditions.

Bony homes

As early as the 19th century, huge heaps of mammoth bones were spotted in parts of Russia, Ukraine and Poland. The bones dated from the Ice Age, and were arranged according to their different shapes. So archaeologists assumed they had been sorted by people of the time preparing mammoth meals for themselves. But, in the 1960s, investigation at Mezhirich in the Ukraine revealed the remains of a hearth underneath the carefully sorted bones.

It became clear that the bones had been stacked up to form the frame of a house. Animal skins were probably draped on top to keep out the freezing winds. As there was very little wood in this region during the Ice Age, the huge bones were one of the only building materials easily available. It seems likely that the mammoths' meat was used for food as well. These mammoth-bone huts have been radiocarbon dated to around 20,000 years ago.

These harpoons and heads, carved from deer antlers and mammoth tusks, come from different sites across Europe. They are between 18,000 and 30,000 years old.

Carving and painting

People in the Ice Age didn't just use animals for food and shelter. Archaeologists have discovered many tools such as harpoons, needles and spear-throwers, carved from mammoth bones and tusks and the bones and antlers of other animals. Some of these artifacts are left plain, but others are engraved with delicate representations of animals. Archaeologists have also found many carvings that don't seem to have had a practical function at all. They are figures of people and animals, carved in a variety of materials including bone, stone and clay, some made as early as 30,000 years ago.

The people of the Ice Age made paintings as well as carvings. When archaeologists first discovered paintings on the walls of caves at Lascaux in France and Altamira in Spain, the paint looked so fresh they thought it must be modern. But on closer inspection, archaeologists discovered Ice Age artifacts, including bone tools and even a piece of rope, still preserved in these caves. They realized the art must be of the same date as the artifacts.

Good vibrations

It's still not known exactly why Ice Age people made paintings and carvings. As much of the surviving art depicts animals, some experts think they were made as part of rituals connected to hunting. But the types of animal bones left over from Ice Age meals do not always match the animals shown in the art, so not all the animals people painted were the same ones they hunted.

Recent research into cave paintings has looked at another possibility. Some archaeologists have noticed that, where the animal paintings cluster thickly, the caves have the best vibrations, producing booming echoes. So perhaps the art was made as part of ceremonies involving music. It certainly must have been important to the people of the Ice Age, as there is evidence they even put up special scaffolding for painting some caves.

Internet links

For a link to a website where you can go on a virtual tour of Lascaux, go to **www.usborne-quicklinks.com**

This painting of a horse dates from around 17,000 years ago. It is in the Painted Gallery at Lascaux, where archaeologists have also noticed very strong echoes.

Stargazers

Some of the most enigmatic monuments in Europe are the massive standing stones, erected from the end of the Stone Age to the beginning of the Bronze Age - between 4000 and 1600BC. Some are arranged in circles and some in lines, while others stand by themselves. Archaeologists have calculated how difficult it must have been for ancient peoples to transport these vast stones with the technology of the time. Nobody knows exactly why they were put there. It's possible they were used in religious ceremonies and recent studies have also found links with astronomy.

This swirling pattern is one of many carved at Newgrange mound in Ireland. These designs may be connected to ancient astronomical uses of the mound.

Sun catchers

At Newgrange in Ireland, stands a huge earth mound set over chambers and a passageway, built of stone slabs. Archaeologists have also found traces of a circle of standing stones. They have now vanished, but they originally stood around the mound. These structures were built around 3200BC by Stone Age peoples who lived by farming.

For just a few days every year around the winter solstice - the shortest day of the year - the rising sun shines through a slot in the roof of the main passage at Newgrange, and illuminates a chamber at the heart of the mound. The builders of Newgrange must have watched the sun's course very carefully to achieve this effect. But no one knows why they may have chosen to commemorate midwinter in this particular way.

Lined up

Archaeologists think that some standing stones were set up, like Newgrange mound, to mark the sun's course. They may have helped people to mark the passing of the seasons accurately and plan their farming activities. But it can be hard to tell just how open-air monuments were connected with astronomy. The sun moves around them all the year, so it's not always obvious which parts of the sun's course they may have been intended to mark. Lines of standing stones at sites such as Carnac in France, dating from around 4000BC, still puzzle archaeologists, but some stone circles have provided clues.

Internet links

For a link to a website where you can see more astronomical alignments at Stonehenge, go to
www.usborne-quicklinks.com

Moon phases

At Stonehenge in England, an ancient path known as the Avenue leads up to the stone circle. Archaeologists realized around 250 years ago that one end of the Avenue is aligned to the midsummer sunrise and the other to the midwinter sunset. Outside the main stone circle, later archaeologists noticed two mounds and two lone standing stones, which form the corners of a rectangle.

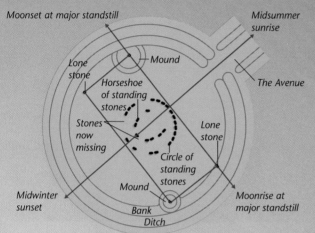

Moonset at major standstill

Midsummer sunrise

Lone stone

Mound

Horseshoe of standing stones

The Avenue

Stones now missing

Lone stone

Circle of standing stones

Mound

Midwinter sunset

Moonrise at major standstill

Bank

Ditch

This plan shows surviving mounds and standing stones at Stonehenge, with some astronomical alignments, explained below. The banks and ditches were built around 2950BC, while the standing stones and mounds date from around 2550-1600BC.

Studying the rectangle formed by the mounds and stones, archaeologists have noticed that its long sides line up with some important stages in the moon's movements across the sky, known as the major standstills. So the builders of Stonehenge may have observed the movements of the moon, as well as the sun.

Harvest calculator

Although the basic alignments at sites like Stonehenge are fairly clear, a recent find from Germany has reminded archaeologists that massive stone monuments weren't strictly necessary for astronomical observations. In 2001, police recovered several Bronze Age artifacts stolen by looters from a 3,600 year old site near the village of Nebra in Germany. Among the objects was a flat circle of bronze, studded with gold bands, dots and what look like a sun and crescent moon. Archaeologists think this object may have been a portable device for keeping track of the positions of the sun and moon.

It seems likely that the gold bands were used to measure midsummer and midwinter sunrises and sunsets. Some of the dots may represent important stars, whose movements are connected with the start of the planting season in this area of Germany. But there are still many unanswered questions about the people of the Bronze and Stone Ages, and their beliefs about the movements of the moon and stars.

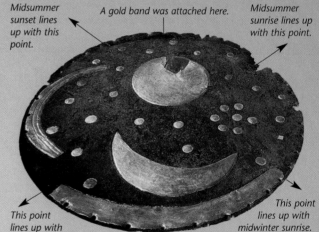

Midsummer sunset lines up with this point.

A gold band was attached here.

Midsummer sunrise lines up with this point.

This point lines up with midwinter sunset.

This point lines up with midwinter sunrise.

This bronze and gold astronomical device was found at Nebra in Germany. It is 30cm (12 in) across and dates from around 1600BC.

This image is from a computer model of Stonehenge, made to help archaeologists study the site's astronomical alignments. It was designed to show movements of the sun, moon and stars at the site.

Athens and Rome

Although the Greek and Roman civilizations flourished more than two thousand years ago, many of their magnificent buildings still stand today. The remains of many more have been excavated and give fascinating information about Greek and Roman art, architecture, engineering and town planning. This rich legacy has had a profound influence on the modern world.

Internet links

For links to websites where you can visit the Forum and the Acropolis, go to www.usborne-quicklinks.com

These are the ruins of the Acropolis, meaning "high city", in Athens as they look today.

This is the Parthenon, the main temple on the Acropolis.

The Propylaea, the gateway to the Acropolis

The city of art

One of the most important ancient Greek sites of all is the city of Athens, which is full of archaeological remains stretching back thousands of years. This great city dominated the Greek world in the Classical period, during the years 500-336BC. Towering over it is the Acropolis, the site of all the important temples to the gods. Excavations over the past 150 years have uncovered detailed information, from which archaeologists have been able to reconstruct what the Acropolis probably once looked like.

This virtual reality reconstruction of the Acropolis has been worked out from information revealed by excavations. You can see the Propylaea at the front, with the Parthenon and other temples behind.

Preservation or plunder?

This is one of the marble panels taken from the Parthenon. It depicts horsemen in a procession and was carved in 438-32BC.

In 1801, British diplomat Lord Elgin obtained permission from the Turkish rulers of Greece to remove some of the sculptures from the Parthenon, which had been left to crumble and decay. These sculptures are now in the British Museum in London and are regarded as among the most famous works of art in the world. Some people think that they should be returned to Greece. But others believe that it would be better to keep them in London where many more people are likely to be able to see them. The sculptures have become a symbol of Greek national pride and a fierce debate is raging between the two sides.

Heart of empire

The ancient Romans conquered all of Italy and created a vast empire stretching across the entire Mediterranean. At the heart of this empire was the city of Rome itself. There are so many layers of remains in the city that it has been described as the most complex archaeological site in the world.

The main part of the city was the Forum, where all the important government buildings and temples were, and this has been the focus of excavations for centuries. One of the most impressive buildings on the edge of the Forum is a huge amphitheatre known as the Colosseum where games took place. Since the mid-1990s, archaeologists have been excavating the basement area. They have been able to calculate how an elaborate system of levers and trapdoors was used to bring wild animals into the arena.

Some of the surviving rooms of Nero's Domus Aurea have painted walls and ceilings. They give some idea of the magnificent decoration inside the palace.

Imperial palaces

The remains of a huge palace were found at the end of the 15th century buried beneath the Colosseum. This was known as the *Domus Aurea*, or Golden House, and it had been built for the emperor Nero in 64-68. The first formal archaeological excavations on the site were started in 1758 and have continued ever since. In 2003, while excavating an area on the edge of the Forum, archaeologists uncovered the foundations of another enormous palace. This had been constructed for the insane emperor Caligula, who was stabbed to death in the year 41.

This picture shows the towering walls of the Colosseum. Inside, were four levels of seating for 50,000 spectators.

Under a blanket of ash

Volcanos are incredibly destructive forces. But volcanic ash can also preserve the ruins of the places that have been destroyed. About 3,500 years ago, a volcano exploded on the Greek island of Thera and a small settlement, now called Akrotiri, was buried beneath ash and lava. 1,500 years later, the Roman town of Pompeii in Italy disappeared under a blanket of ash when Mount Vesuvius erupted.

Time stands still

Archaeologists have been excavating the site of Akrotiri since 1967. They have uncovered complete streets of standing houses, some with wonderful wall-paintings still as fresh and bright as the day the volcano erupted. But mysteriously there are no signs of the people themselves. Archaeologists believe that they must have had some warning and were able to get away before the volcano exploded.

End of a civilization?

One of Europe's earliest civilizations developed from about 2000BC on the island of Crete, 110km (70 miles) to the south of Thera. Remains were first discovered there in the early 20th century by British archaeologist Arthur Evans, who named it the Minoan civilization after King Minos, a legendary ruler of Crete. Some archaeologists thought that the explosion on Thera may also have caused the collapse of the Minoan civilization. But by analysing samples of volcanic ash, archaeologists have been able to prove that Akrotiri was abandoned at least 20 years before the Cretan cities were destroyed. The causes of the end of the Minoan civilization still remain a mystery.

Archaeological excavations at Akrotiri uncovered superb wall-paintings, such as this one of a fisherman and his catch.

Killed in their tracks

The people of Akrotiri were probably able to escape before their village was destroyed. But the people of the Roman town of Pompeii in Italy weren't so lucky. One August day in the year 79, Mount Vesuvius suddenly erupted, sending a great cloud of deadly ash and poisonous gases shooting up into the sky. Molten lava poured down the mountainside. At the foot of the volcano lay the town, which was soon smothered by the ash.

The Pompeiians ran in all directions, trying in vain to escape the deadly tide. But they were quickly overcome and buried under the ash. And there they lay for the next 1,800 years.

This plaster cast shows the dying moments of a dog in Pompeii.

Raising the dead

The remains of Pompeii were discovered in 1710, but formal excavations didn't start until 1860. Since then, archaeologists have found entire streets of houses and their contents. They have also found hundreds of cavities in the solid ash, created by the bodies of the people who had been killed.

In 1864, Giuseppe Fiorelli, the archaeologist in charge of the excavation, developed a clever method of recreating the bodies. He poured plaster into the cavities, which set hard in the shape of the bodies. Today, a transparent substance is used, allowing any bones and objects such as rings to be seen.

This sequence shows Giuseppe Fiorelli's method of reconstructing the bodies.

The person collapses and is buried under volcanic ash.

The body decays, leaving a cavity around the skeleton.

Archaeologists pour plaster into the cavity.

The ash around the cavity acts as a cast and the plaster hardens to form the shape of the body. The ash is then chipped away.

Internet links

For links to websites where you can explore Akrotiri and read more about the eruption that hit Pompeii, go to **www.usborne-quicklinks.com**

This is a view of Pompeii today. Now archaeologists are excavating the foundations of the buildings, to find out more about the development of the city.

The Coppergate dig

Many European cities have been lived in for thousands of years. New houses and roads are piled on top of older ones, so that layers of history lie buried beneath the modern streets. Archaeologists working in York, in northern England, have uncovered evidence from every period since the Romans settled there in the year 71. But in cities like York it can often be difficult to get at remains, because modern buildings are standing in the way.

This iron and copper helmet, dating from 750-775, was found just as developers were moving in at Coppergate, York. Excavations at Coppergate unearthed artifacts from every period of York's history.

Mapping through the ages

Even a modern map of York gives many clues about the city's past, as the plans below show. Some of the city walls and streets still follow the Roman grid pattern, while others have Viking names: Micklegate means "big street" and Coppergate, "street of the cup-makers". This helps identify areas that may contain archaeological remains. But archaeologists still have to wait for an opportunity to investigate.

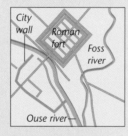

This plan shows Roman York, around the year 300. It is based on Roman archaeological finds.

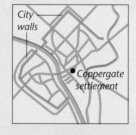

This plan is based on finds from the Viking era. It shows York around 1000, at the end of Viking occupation.

This plan of modern York shows that some walls and streets still follow Viking and Roman routes.

These Viking beads found at Coppergate are evidence of the Vikings' trade, as well as their craft activities. The orange beads, made of amber, were imported from Scandinavia.

Jorvik Viking city

In 1976, the local council demolished a pub and a sweet factory on Coppergate to make room for a car park. Archaeologists suspected the site might conceal Viking remains, so they persuaded the council to let them investigate. But they had no idea of the scale of what awaited them.

Digging down through the layers, they found an entire street from around the year 900, the period when Viking settlers lived in York - or Jorvik, as they called the city. Viking houses had been found elsewhere in Europe and even at one site in the USA. But the detail and quantity of evidence discovered at Coppergate is unique.

The damp conditions of the site preserved wood, leather and fabric, as well as human skeletons. Remains of houses and debris from household waste, craft and cooking were all still there. Waste pits revealed fruit and vegetable seeds, fish and animal bones and human parasites, showing what the diet and health of the Viking residents was like. The archaeologists even found some of the wooden cups that gave the street its Viking name.

This virtual reconstruction shows how the Viking street at Coppergate probably looked around the year 900.

Race against time

Over five years, archaeologists worked down though 9m (around 18ft) of soil and removed hundreds of thousands of finds, going right back to the period when the Romans lived in York. There's now a popular visitor attraction at Coppergate, where you can see artifacts from the dig and visit a reconstruction of the Viking street, complete with sounds and even smells.

The archaeologists working at Coppergate were lucky, as they managed to raise enough money for a thorough dig. But many digs in towns and cities are much more rushed. Archaeologists have to work against the clock to recover as much as possible, before the bulldozers move in and destroy the remains, or cover them up for another hundred years or so.

Internet links

For a link to a website where you can explore artifacts from Coppergate, go to **www.usborne-quicklinks.com**

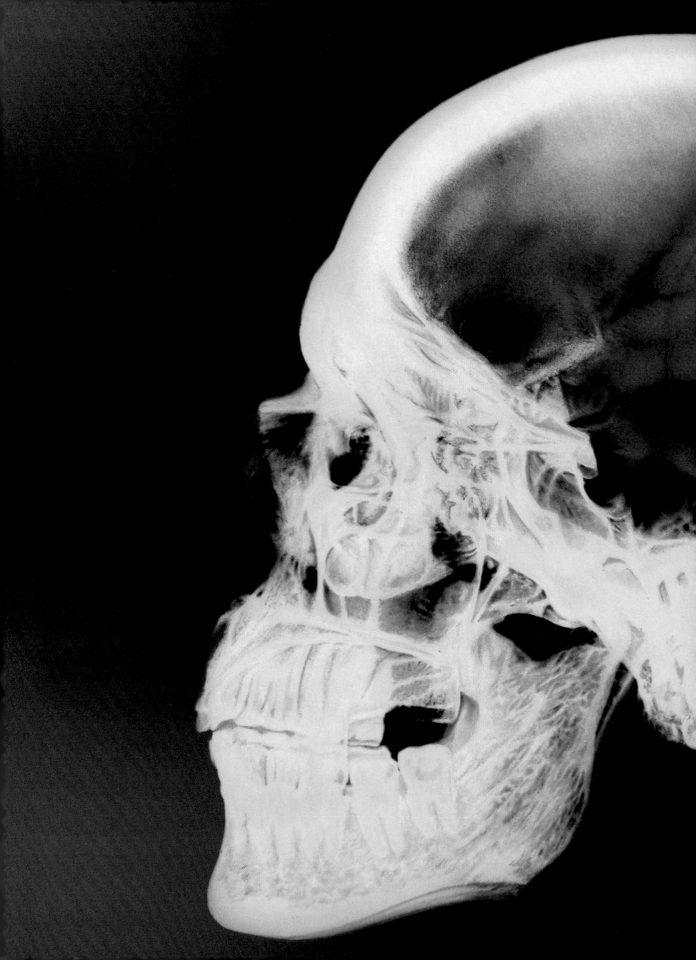

ARCHAEOLOGY FACT FILE

Here you can find out more about the latest
techniques for dating, interpreting and
preserving archaeological finds. You can also
compare famous sites, finds and
archaeologists on a timeline of archaeology
and check unfamiliar words in a glossary.

This image is an X-ray of a well-preserved Roman skull from the city of Gloucester in England.

Codebreakers

Written records from the past provide essential clues for archaeologists, but trying to read them can be like cracking a code. It's a double challenge to decipher the writing system and to identify the language it represents. Many ancient languages have died out completely, and so they can't be identified, while different writing systems, also known as scripts, can be very complex. Against all these odds, some experts from around the world have succeeded. You can read about their stories here.

The Rosetta Stone, dating from 196BC, was discovered in Rosetta (Rashid) in Egypt, by French soldiers serving under Napoleon, in 1799. They were digging out old stones to use in strengthening a fort.

Written in stone

For centuries, people were puzzled by symbols carved on ancient Egyptian monuments. Were they patterns, pictures or symbols? What could they mean? Ancient Greek writings mentioned an Egyptian script known as hieroglyphics, meaning "sacred writing". But it wasn't clear how it worked or what language the ancient Egyptians had spoken. Then, in 1799, a slab of black stone was discovered near Rosetta in Egypt. It had three bands of writing on it, one in Greek, one in Egyptian hieroglyphics and one in another Egyptian script called Demotic. Less than 30 years later, hieroglyphics were deciphered.

Internet links

For a link to a website where you can explore many different ancient scripts, go to
www.usborne-quicklinks.com

Some Egyptian hieroglyphs, showing the sound each symbol represents

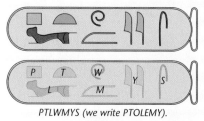

PTLWMYS (we write PTOLEMY).

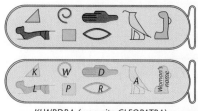

KLWPDRA (we write CLEOPATRA).

Thomas Young, a linguist, guessed correctly that the three scripts on the stone said the same thing. Translating the Greek version, he noticed several names. He realized that some of the symbols in the hieroglyphic text, set in oval frames called cartouches, might be the same names. One sequence matched the name of Pharaoh Ptolemy, with a symbol for each sound except the vowels. But Young couldn't make out what language the hieroglyphic text was written in.

Another scholar named Jean-Francois Champollion wasn't put off so easily. He tried spelling out hieroglyphic words using Young's system, and soon found some that sounded similar to Coptic, a language still spoken in parts of Egypt. This was a revelation. He quickly discovered that, although some hieroglyphs were sound signs, others were "sounds like" symbols: this is like drawing a picture of an eye for the sound "i". This final breakthrough, made in 1824, cracked the hieroglyph code.

This Mycenaean clay tablet, unearthed at the Cretan palace of Knossos, lists offerings to different gods. It is written in Linear B script.

This carving is from a Maya temple at Copan in Honduras. It shows a ruler seated on glyphs that spell out details about his life.

Taking the tablets

A people called the Mycenaeans lived in parts of mainland Greece from around 2,000BC and ruled the island of Crete until 1,375BC. Their writing, known as Linear B, survives on several hundred clay tablets. But few people thought it would ever be deciphered. As there were no other clues, a linguist named Alice Kober tried breaking down the script into mathematical formulas. She calculated how often each sign appeared in surviving Linear B documents, and in which order. This told her that most of the signs must represent syllables - short sounds made up of a vowel and one or more consonants. But Kober died in 1950, without ever finding out what language the script represented.

Maya mystery

The Maya language is still spoken in parts of Central America, but knowledge of Maya writing died out after the Spanish conquest in the 16th century. A Christian priest, Diego de Landa, recorded some of the Maya script in around 1560. He assumed it was an alphabet and asked some surviving Maya scribes to write down the signs for "a", "b", "c", and so on. But, centuries later, when archaeologists tried to use de Landa's list to read Maya inscriptions, they couldn't get it to fit. They realized that de Landa had not been exactly right in thinking the script was an alphabet.

Michael Ventris, a keen amateur linguist, was fascinated by Kober's work, and tried matching different sounds to the signs. He found several combinations that resembled ancient Greek words. This was a total surprise, but in 1953, Ventris proved that Linear B is the earliest identified form of Greek.

Some Maya glyphs, showing the sounds they represent

PAKAL (means SHIELD)

HUBI (means DESTRUCTION)

In 1952, Yuri Knorozov discovered that the signs (known as glyphs) stood for syllables, not letters. He identified glyphs that spelled out several words in the Maya language, but other signs remained a mystery. Later, Tatiana Proskouriakoff realized that many of the inscriptions on Maya buildings listed names and dates, and were not normal words at all. But some signs are still undeciphered and work on Maya glyphs continues.

Mycenaean Linear B script

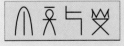

TI RI PO DE
TRIPODES (means TRIPODS)

A KO SO NE
AKSONES (means AXES)

The restored palace of Knossos on Crete, where many Mycenaean clay tablets were found

Historical dating

Until scientific dating techniques were introduced in the early 20th century, archaeologists had to try to work out the age of sites by using ancient calendars and written records. This method, known as historical dating, is still very useful today. But, to make sense, any historical dating system has to be reasonably complete, and archaeologists have to be able to tie it in with modern dating systems.

Star gazing

Like many ancient peoples, the Egyptians used their knowledge of the sun, moon and stars to work out several calendars. They noticed that at the same time every year, the star Sirius disappeared below the horizon, and reappeared just before sunrise 70 days later. This happened just when the waters of the River Nile began to rise for the annual floods, and this important event came to mark the date of the Egyptian New Year.

365 days a year

Later, the Egyptians were the first to divide the year into 365 days. This division was based on the time it takes for the earth to move around the sun, known as a solar year. But since there are 365.25 days in a solar year, their calendar gradually slipped out of step with the New Year as calculated from the first sighting of Sirius.

The Roman leader Julius Caesar improved on the Egyptian calendar by adding an extra day in February every four years. This is the Leap Year we have today. This version, known as the Julian calendar, was still 11 minutes and 14 seconds too long so that it gradually fell out of line with the seasons. In 1582, Pope Gregory XIII solved the problem by introducing further minor changes. His Gregorian calendar is now used in most countries throughout the world.

This wall painting is in the tomb of the Egyptian pharaoh Seti I (1306-1290BC), which was discovered in 1817 by Giovanni Belzoni. It shows constellations (groups of stars) in the form of gods.

Starting over again

Instead of counting the years continuously from a set date as we do, the Egyptians used a cyclical calendar, counting the years from the accession of each king. When a new king came to the throne, they started all over again at year 1. By referring to surviving official records known as king lists, archaeologists know who reigned, in what order and for how long. They can add up the reign dates and then tie them in with our present dating system.

Internet links

For a link to a website where you can convert dates to the Muslim calendar and find out more about the Maya calendar, go to **www.usborne-quicklinks.com**

The Maya calendar

Another example of a cyclical calendar was developed by the Maya people of Central America. This was based on a 52-year cycle known as the Calendar Round. They used it to record important events, giving the year, month and even the day of the week. In the 1950s, after years of research, archaeologists began to understand the symbols the Maya used in their calendar. Once they were able to do that, they could begin to work out their history.

How did it work?

The Maya calendar was based on two cycles: the Sacred Round of 260 days, and the Haab or solar year of 365 days. The Sacred Round consisted of two sequences: 13 numbered days, and 20 named days. Together they made a cycle of 260 days (13x20).

This diagram shows how the sequences fitted together. They worked rather like a set of interlocking wheels.

Each of these spokes represents one of 13 numbered days.

Each of these spokes represents one of 20 named days.

The 260-day cycle began with 1 Imix, 2 Ik, 3 Akbal, and so on until it reached 13 Ben. Then the number sequence began again with 1 Ix, 2 Men and so on. After the 260th day, 13 Ahaw, the whole cycle started all over again with 1 Imix.

The Haab year consisted of 18 months of 20 days each, making 360 days in total. The Maya then added a short month of 5 days at the end of each year to make it add up to 365 days. The Haab cycle interlocked with the Sacred Round and the two moved round simultaneously. After 52 years (18,980 days) the whole cycle began again.

Moving straight on

One of the first people to use a linear calendar - which starts at a fixed date and extends from that time - were the ancient Greeks, who dated everything from the first Olympic Games. The western Christian calendar, which is the one we use today, starts from the birth of Jesus Christ. The Muslim calendar is dated from the Hejira, the journey of the Prophet Mohammed from Mecca to Medina. This date corresponds to 622 on the Christian calendar. The year 2000 on the Christian calendar is 1421 on the Muslim calendar.

Seasonal dating

The passage of time and the seasons affects the growth of plants and animals and leaves tiny traces in their bodies. Archaeologists can use these as clues to work out the age of ancient sites.

If you look closely, you can see the individual rings.

Tree-ring dating

Most trees produce a ring of new wood each year. These rings are wider in warm, wet years and narrower in cold, dry years. These wide and narrow bands build up into a distinctive pattern of growth rings.

The ring of new wood forms on the outside of the trunk, just beneath the outer layer of bark.

In the early 20th century, a scientist named Andrew Douglass used this information to develop a dating system known as dendrochronology. Archaeologists use it to calculate the date of wood by studying its growth rings. This is useful for dating the remains of wooden buildings, ships or other objects made from wood.

If archaeologists know the date a tree was cut down, they know the exact year in which the outermost growth ring formed. This gives them an end date for that tree's growth rings. Trees of the same species, growing in the same region, show similar patterns of ring widths. So archaeologists can match up the ring width pattern of a dated tree with that of other trees. The matching rings will have grown in the same year. If they can match up patterns from successively older trees, they can build up a dated master pattern going back hundreds, even thousands of years. Wood found at archaeological sites can then be compared with the master pattern, to date it.

Here is an imaginary master pattern of tree rings.

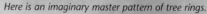

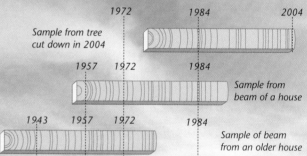

Sample from tree cut down in 2004

1972   1984   2004

1957   1972   1984

Sample from beam of a house

1943   1957   1972   1984

Sample of beam from an older house

When wood samples from archaeological sites are matched and overlapped, archaeologists can extend the dating back into prehistory. A number of master patterns have been constructed for different parts of the world. One of the longest is the pattern for Europe, which is based on the remains of Irish oak trees and stretches back to around 5500BC.

Laying down layers

Archaeologists also look for yearly patterns in other places. For example, melting glaciers deposit layers of sediment, known as varves, on the edge of lakes. This has been happening since the end of the last Ice Age.

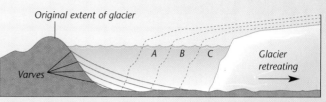

Original extent of glacier

Varves

A B C

Glacier retreating

This diagram shows how melting glaciers retreat and create yearly varves. When the ice retreats to position A, the mud and rock carried in the melted ice forms the bottom varve.

Each year (B, C and so on), more debris is deposited. The thickness of each varve shows how much of the glacier has melted, giving an idea of the environmental conditions.

Over the years, more and more varves are laid down. Like tree-rings, the varves vary in thickness from year to year. A thick varve results from increased melting in warm weather, while a thin one is formed in colder conditions when the ice melts less.

Scientists have recorded sequences of varves from several glacial lakes. By counting the number of varves in each lake, they can work out the age of the lake. They have linked a number of these sequences together to produce one continuous sequence stretching back 13,000 years, from the present to the time when the first ice sheets started melting. This gives them a reasonably accurate date for the end of the last Ice Age. The sequence serves as a useful guide to help date local archaeological sites. It also gives vital information about weather conditions over thousands of years. By knowing this, archaeologists can work out what sorts of plants and animals would have lived there and how many people would have lived in the area.

This cross-section through a glacier shows layers of rocks and mud swept up and frozen into the glacier. When this debris is deposited in lakes, it forms layers known as varves.

The magnificent Moreno Glacier has been slowly moving through the mountains of Patagonia in Argentina for thousands of years. Like a huge frozen river, it eventually pours into a glacial lake.

Internet links

For a link to a website where you can find out the latest news about tree-ring dating, go to **www.usborne-quicklinks.com**

Radioactive dating

Archaeologists can make use of one of the most common activities in the natural world for dating purposes: radioactive decay. Radioactive chemical elements found in plant and animal remains, pottery, and even in rocks, form the basis of several modern archaeological dating methods.

Radioactive clocks

The radioactive forms of elements, such as carbon and potassium, are unstable, which means they tend to decay, giving off energy and radiation. Each element decays at a certain rate, and scientists can use this knowledge to work out how old an object is, if they know what it is made of. The rate of decay is called a "half-life", which means the time it takes for half the element to decay. Different elements have different half-lives, from a few seconds to thousands of years. For example, one type of carbon has a half-life of 5,730 years, while the half-life of one variety of potassium is about 1.3 billion years.

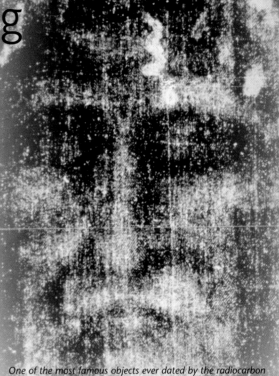

One of the most famous objects ever dated by the radiocarbon method is the Turin Shroud, which for centuries many people have believed to be the burial shroud of Jesus Christ. But, in 1988, radiocarbon dating revealed that it may have been made much later, during the 15th century.

Carbon countdown

Radiocarbon dating is based on the rate of decay of the radioactive form of carbon, known as carbon-14 (C14). It was first used in the 1950s, and meant that, for the first time, plant and animal remains could be dated scientifically, as far back as 70,000 years. At first, radiocarbon dating was not very precise, but much more accurate dates can now be achieved by adjusting the results to take into account climatic information obtained from tree-ring dating.

Ticking away

Plants absorb C14 during photosynthesis, the process they use to make food. Animals take it in when they eat the plants. But it decays as fast as plants and animals take it in, so the level of C14 inside them stays about the same. When they die, the C14 inside their remains continues to decay. But now they are not taking in any more and the level goes down. Scientists can measure how much of the original C14 is left. As they know how long C14 takes to decay (it has a half-life of 5,730 years), they can work out how old the remains are.

These diagrams show how carbon-14 is formed and decays.

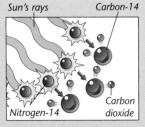

C14 is produced when the sun's rays hit nitrogen-14 atoms in the atmosphere. Some form radioactive carbon dioxide.

Plants absorb some of this radioactive carbon dioxide. Animals take in C14 when they eat the plants.

When the plants and animals die, the C14 in them decays and they do not take in any more. The level of C14 goes down.

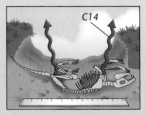

Scientists then take a small sample of the remains and use special equipment to measure the C14 still remaining.

Making tracks

Fission-track measurement is used to date rocks and objects, such as glass and pottery, that contain uranium minerals and were made using extreme heat. This works by counting the microscopic tracks made during the fission (splitting) of a radioactive form of uranium called U238. This process starts as soon as the object begins to cool down after the firing process in its manufacture. The rate of fission is constant, so the age of the material since the fission tracks began can be calculated.

Internet links

For a link to a website where you can see photographs of uranium fission tracks, go to www.usborne-quicklinks.com

Fission-track measurement can be used to date glass objects less than 2,000 years old, such as these fragments of a 4th-century German glass bowl.

Rock clock

Potassium-argon (K-Ar) dating is based on the decay of a radioactive form of potassium, known as potassium-40 (K40), to form the gas argon-40 (Ar40). Potassium-40 is found in rocks, so K-Ar dating is used to date the rocks that contain ancient objects, rather than the objects themselves. When archaeologists know the age of the rocks, this tells them the age of any objects inside the rocks. Geologists have used this method to date volcanic rocks at sites in East Africa, such as Olduvai Gorge, which contain fossils of early human ancestors.

The rocks of Olduvai Gorge in Tanzania, below, were formed at least 4 million years ago, at the same time as our earliest ancestors were living there. Archaeologists have been working in the area since the 1930s.

Dating with light

Thermoluminescence (TL) dating is another method of dating pottery, used since the mid-1960s. After firing, energy from the decay of radioactive elements in the clay is trapped. This builds up as the years pass. When the pottery is recovered by archaeologists, sometimes thousands of years later, scientists take a sample by drilling out a tiny amount. They heat this up, and trapped energy is released as light. By measuring the strength of the light, the scientists can calculate how long ago the pot was fired.

This ancient pottery figure from northwestern Iran was dated to the early 1st millenium BC using thermoluminescence dating.

Preserving the past

The artifacts excavated by archaeologists have to be preserved so that they do not decay any further. This is called conservation and the work is done in laboratories by scientists called conservators. Their methods depend on what the object is made of, where it was found and how badly it has decayed.

First aid

Organic materials, such as wood, fabric and human remains, are very fragile and often start to decay the moment they are exposed to the air. If this happens, they need immediate "first aid" on site until they can be properly treated. The body of Ötzi the Iceman was buried in a glacier for more than 5,000 years. After it was removed, it was kept frozen and now has to be stored in a special cold chamber at -6° Celsius (21° Fahrenheit), the same temperature as the glacier. Ötzi can only be taken out to be examined for 20 minutes every two weeks.

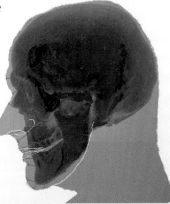

Ötzi's appearance has been reconstructed here by using a computer to "stretch" a face over his skull.

Waterlogged

Organic materials that have absorbed water become soft and very weak. Wood and leather objects removed from wet conditions are often sprayed with polyethylene glycol. This is a liquid wax that slowly replaces the water and then hardens and strengthens the object. A quicker way of preserving waterlogged organic materials is by freeze-drying - the same process used to make instant coffee.

Pottery puzzles

Pottery is one of the most common materials found on archaeological digs. Because so many pieces are recovered, only the most complete pots are restored. After cleaning the pieces, the conservator carefully sticks them together, using a special glue that dissolves easily. This ensures the pot is not damaged.

Moving mountains

Archaeological sites themselves are constantly under threat from new building work, mining, farming and even war. Once excavated, they are exposed to the elements and often to tens of thousands of visiting tourists, too. Sites have to be managed so that all these pressures do not damage them.

One of the biggest ever conservation projects was the rescue and resiting of the enormous temples of Abu Simbel in Egypt. This was organized by UNESCO (United Nations Educational Scientific and Cultural Organization). Work began in 1964 to save the sandstone temples, which would have been drowned under the waters of a lake behind the new Aswan dam. Over the next four years, they were cut up into more than a thousand blocks and moved up 60m (200ft) to higher ground where they were reassembled.

Internet links

For a link to a website where you can see more pictures of Abu Simbel, go to **www.usborne-quicklinks.com**

Conserving metal

Most metals have corroded badly by the time they are unearthed. They react with oxygen to form metal oxides, such as iron oxide (rust), which break down the structure of the metal. But conservators can do a lot to remove the corrosion and prevent any more damage. Before any conservation work starts, metal artifacts are often X-rayed to find out what lies beneath the corrosion.

This is an Iron Age skull and headdress dating to around 200BC, found at Deal in England.

This X-ray of the headdress shows the fine decoration beneath the corrosion.

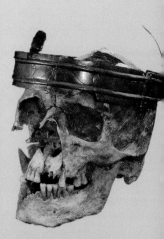

This is the headdress and skull after the conservation work was completed.

The metal can be cleaned with a jet of tiny hard particles, then soaked in hot distilled water to remove any corrosive salts. Sometimes the corrosion is carefully scraped off with a scalpel under a microscope. The process of decay cannot be reversed, but if the object is properly stored after cleaning and conservation, any further decay can usually be prevented.

Conservation experts used lifting equipment to reassemble the huge blocks of stone of the Abu Simbel temples in their new location.

A face from the past

When archaeologists discover ancient human remains, a few bits of bone are often all they have to go on. Scientific tests on bones can detect evidence of the health and eating habits of the dead person. But if a skull survives, it's possible to reconstruct the face and bring the dry bones back to life.

Skull beneath the skin

People's bones help to shape the outer layers of muscles and skin, affecting the way they look. By measuring thousands of people's heads, scientists have found some general rules about how the shape of a skull affects a face. Although these rules aren't 100% accurate for every person, they give archaeologists a good idea of how someone's face looked, just from the shape of their skull.

Mirror image

Face reconstructions can sometimes help archaeologists put a name to a body. This only works in a few rare cases, where there's a good idea of who the remains may have belonged to, as well as a fairly accurate surviving portrait of that person. If the shape of the face in the portrait matches the face reconstruction closely, it is probably the same person. If they don't match, it usually means that the portrait was not very accurate, or that the remains belong to someone else.

This wooden sculpture of Tutankhamun was found in his tomb. It is one of several portraits of the pharaoh, and helps archaeologists reconstruct his appearance.

Internet links

For a link to a website where you can find out more about Tutankhamun's virtual face and see more pictures, go to **www.usborne-quicklinks.com**

Face to face

The usual way of reconstructing a face is fairly low-tech, involving plaster casts, clay, and many hours of painstaking work. These diagrams show the different stages.

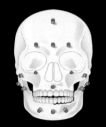

Measuring pegs are fitted to a cast of the skull, to mark the depth of the features on top.

The layers of the face are built up out of clay. Some features, like the nose, are guesswork.

Glass eyes are fitted and the skin texture is added to the topmost layer.

Finally, hair and ears are attached and the surface is painted in flesh tones.

The mummy returns

Computer technology has helped reconstruct a face for the Egyptian pharaoh Tutankhamun. No one is now allowed to examine Tutankhamun's body, but old X-rays of his head were used to get skull measurements. The likely contours of his face were laid on top, then skin texture was added.

The old X-rays weren't very clear, so this reconstruction involved a lot of guesswork and doesn't look very like surviving portraits of the pharaoh. But the reconstruction also revealed new medical evidence. Scientists found traces in the old X-rays of a rare disease that made the pharaoh vulnerable to injuries, and some marks suggesting he'd had a serious fall. Perhaps this is why Tutankhamun died aged only 18.

High-tech tricks

The latest technology can also help with face reconstruction, especially in cases where shrivelled facial tissues or mummy wrappings still cover the remains. Scientists use CAT scans or X-rays to "see" through the wrappings and measure the skull underneath. They feed this information into a computer, which creates a virtual skull and makes a face to fit, using the same average measurements that more traditional reconstructors use.

This is a CAT scan image of a mummy's face.

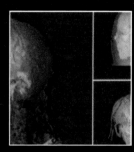

Here you can see the skull underneath the skin.

This is a virtual reconstruction of Tutankhamun's face, made using the latest computer technology.

Fakes and forgeries

People have been making forgeries of ancient artifacts for centuries, usually to pass them off as genuine antiquities. The latest materials and methods make it possible to produce perfect casts and copies. Experts and archaeologists try to keep one step ahead of the forgers, but the quality of the copies is often so good that sometimes even the experts are fooled.

Horse trials

Scientific tests, such as thermoluminescence (TL) dating, can help experts prove whether an object is genuine or a fake by dating it. When Chinese archaeologists found pottery horses from the T'ang period (618-906), they also discovered one of the original casts used to make them. Soon, hundreds of copies of the horses were being passed off as genuine. It was very difficult to tell the difference with the naked eye, but TL dating showed which were fakes by revealing when they were made.

Crystal clear

Powerful microscopes can show up all sorts of interesting details on the surface of suspect objects. For many years a rock crystal skull was believed to have been carved by the Aztec people of Central America some time before the 16th century. But when scientists examined the skull under a microscope, they discovered that the surface had been cut and polished with a cutting wheel. This was a 19th-century European technique that would have been unknown to the Aztecs.

This crystal skull was once thought to have been carved by the Aztecs. When viewed under a microscope, the marks left by the cutting wheel told experts that the skull had not been made by the Aztecs and that it must be a fake.

Internet links

For links to websites where you can see more pictures of the fake princess and Piltdown Man, go to **www.usborne-quicklinks.com**

Suspicious ingredients

A technique known as neutron activation analysis (NAA) can identify the chemicals present in a wide range of materials, such as flint, pottery and metals. NAA can show tiny chemical differences between modern and old metals. This is very useful in detecting fakes, because certain chemicals were only added to some metals, such as brass, after a certain date.

Electrons and X-rays

Scanning electron microscopes (SEM) produce very detailed images and can be used to prove whether or not something is a fake. The object is scanned with a beam of electrons, which produces an image so clear it is possible to see exactly how it was made. At the same time, the electron scan causes the object to emit X-rays which can be analysed to determine its chemical composition. This can reveal how old it is and whether it is genuine or a fake.

In 2000, a collection of gold necklaces and brooches was found in a field near Winchester in southern England. When experts studied them by SEM, the fine decoration and the purity of the gold revealed that they had probably been made in Rome. They may have been presented to a British chieftain just before or after the Roman conquest of Britain.

Central clasp of one of the gold necklaces found near Winchester in England

This cluster of tiny gold balls is shown in detail in the SEM image below.

This SEM image of the clasp on the necklace tells archaeologists more about how and where it was made.

The missing link?

One of the most famous archaeological hoaxes was that of the so-called Piltdown Man. In 1912, fragments of a human skull with an ape-like jawbone were found at Piltdown, a small village in Sussex. This led to excited claims that the "missing link" between modern humans and our ape-like ancestors had been found. But in 1953, Piltdown Man was proved to be a fake. By measuring the amount of fluorine, uranium and nitrogen in the bones, experts discovered that the skull was only about 620 years old. The jawbone was even more recent and came from an orang-utan.

The fake princess

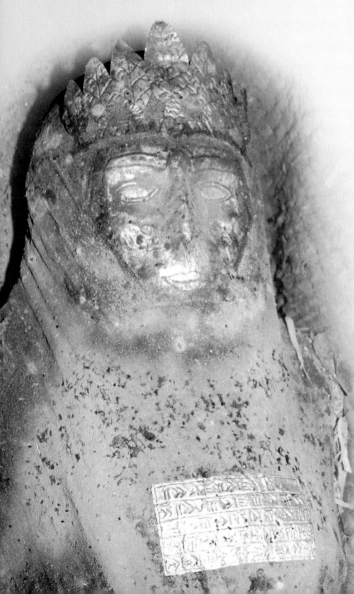

In 2000, what seemed like an amazing discovery was made when a mummy turned up in a remote part of western Pakistan. At first, archaeologists believed it was the 2,600 year-old body of a Persian princess. But experts became suspicious when they saw mistakes in the ancient writing on the mummy case. When they examined the mummy itself, they discovered it was less than four years old. They were even more shocked to discover that the woman who had been mummified may also have been murdered.

This is the wooden case of the fake mummy. Archaeologists soon discovered that it was not what it seemed.

Fact or fiction?

As this book shows, archaeologists don't just set out to find evidence about the past - they try to understand what they find as well. But two archaeologists looking at the same artifact or site may come up with completely different theories about who used it, and how and when they did so. Explanations also change over time, as new evidence is discovered and ideas and attitudes change. So, in the end, you have to decide for yourself whether the facts fit the theories.

These are stone tools, dating from around 20,000 to 40,000BC. When artifacts like these were first discovered, no one knew what they were.

The cutting edge

Even before archaeologists began to study objects from the past, people were aware of the great ruins of previous civilizations and found mysterious objects buried underground. They often didn't know what they were or how they had got there. So, to explain them, they made up stories about giants building massive structures and fairies burying enchanted treasure. Archaeologists set out to discover the facts behind these legends. But even for world-famous sites that have been studied for centuries, there's still plenty of debate. For example, no one really knows what Stonehenge was built for, though there have been hundreds of different theories.

Internet links

For a link to a website where you can look at 3-D images of many more ancient stone balls, go to **www.usborne-quicklinks.com**

Even with simple artifacts, you can't take anything for granted. Thousands of shaped stones have been discovered at sites around the world. Archaeologists now agree that they were tools for cutting and scraping, made by early people thousands of years ago. But this has only been accepted in the last 200 years. Before that, some people thought they were natural objects, caused by thunderstorms. Even now, not all the problems have been solved. Some stone tools look as if they have never been used. Were they made for display, and if so, why? Or were they simply lost before anyone had a chance to use them? It's possible archaeologists of the future may come up with a convincing explanation.

This huge stone enclosure is known as Great Zimbabwe. Archaeologists now know who built it, but in the past this was the focus of much debate.

This is part of a tourist resort that claims to have recreated the mythical city of Atlantis. There's no archaeological evidence such a city ever existed, but this doesn't stop some people from believing the legends.

Mad, bad and dangerous

Obviously, some interpretations will be proved wrong by advances in technology, or even just by changes in attitudes. That's what happened at Great Zimbabwe, a huge stone-built enclosure in modern Zimbabwe. Many people, including some early excavators there, thought the structure was too impressive to have been made by African people. This interpretation was based on nothing more than outdated, racist attitudes. Later archaeologists looked carefully at the evidence in and around the site, and showed that Great Zimbabwe was built by the black African Shona people, who lived there from 1100 to 1500.

There are some people, mostly not trained archaeologists, who still choose to ignore archaeological evidence and fantasize about ancient sites and artifacts. The idea that aliens made the Nazca Lines in Peru, or that people from the mythical city of Atlantis built the Egyptian pyramids, have replaced the old legends of giants and fairies. There's no evidence whatsoever for any of these claims, so you could see them as harmless fun. But they take the credit away from the ancient people who really built these impressive monuments.

You decide

Because of difficulties like these, archaeologists are very careful to take all the evidence into account when they are formulating theories about a particular site, artifact or culture. By comparing all the different information they can try to ensure they don't take anything for granted, or ignore anything. This gives them the best chance of coming up with an explanation that fits the evidence.

But sometimes there are just no convincing explanations on offer. Some archaeological finds are so mysterious, it's anyone's guess what they were. Hundreds of carved stone balls have been discovered in the northeast of Scotland. They date from around 3000-2000BC, but no one has any idea what they were for. What do you think?

Each of these ancient stone balls is around the size of a tennis ball. They must have taken hours to carve, but what were they for?

Dangerous times

Archaeologists can now find out more about the past than ever before, yet ancient remains are increasingly under threat. Sites around the world are being stripped and vital archaeological evidence destroyed by people wanting to own ancient artifacts. Even everyday tourists can cause problems. Some of the world's most famous archaeological sites are being closed to prevent damage caused by visitors. Archaeologists are now looking to the future, as well as the past.

Internet links

For a link to a website where you can see pictures of artifacts missing from the Iraq Museum, go to **www.usborne-quicklinks.com**

This photograph shows an American tank protecting the Iraq Museum, during the Iraq war in 2003. Unfortunately, many of the museum's unique artifacts had already been looted.

Black market

Today, archaeology is the focus of great interest all over the world. This is often a great boost for archaeologists, helping them gain funding and public support for their work. But, sadly, it can also create problems, as demand for ancient artifacts soars. Private collectors and museums pay top prices for rare finds, but some do not care where the objects come from. This can tempt unscrupulous dealers to acquire artifacts illegally, by looting or stealing them from archaeologial sites or museums.

Looting of archaeological sites has been going on since ancient times. Even the ancient Egyptian pharaohs tried to hide and protect their tombs, knowing that looters were ready and waiting to seize their rich grave goods. Despite international efforts to deter collectors from buying illegally acquired artifacts, looting is still going on today. It is often carried out on a grand scale by well-organized, armed gangs that are dangerous and difficult to catch.

Smash and grab

Unlike archaeologists, who record the position and state of everything they find, looters are only interested in uncovering artifacts they can sell easily. They rip through any other finds, including human remains, destroying vital evidence about the date and use of the site. Even if archaeologists manage to recover looted artifacts, they can never recreate the lost archaeological information that lay buried with them.

Some recent examples are particularly shocking. During the war in Iraq in 2003, looters hacked into the area's most important archaeological sites, and museums were stripped bare. At some Native American sites in the USA, a legal loophole has allowed entrepreneurs to bulldoze layers of delicate Mimbres pottery in order to extract a few unbroken pots. In Europe, too, many digs are being raided at night by criminal gangs who wait for archaeologists to start digging and then snatch any artifacts.

This pot was made by the Mimbres people of the American Southwest. Many Mimbres sites have been bulldozed in the search for similar pots.

Killing with kindness

This kind of looting is very dramatic, but great damage can also be caused by archaeology lovers. Thousands of enthusiasts around the world use metal detectors in their spare time, to find buried objects. Though many act responsibly, reporting historic finds to local archaeologists, others tear artifacts out of the ground and keep them, without appreciating how much this can damage the archaeology of the site.

This diver is using a metal detector to search a wreck site. Thousands of metal artifacts are found this way every year, but not all are reported.

Even tourists visiting archaeological sites can cause damage, whether they mean to or not. Climbing on ancient ruins or taking small artifacts home as souvenirs may not sound serious, but if every visitor did this, there would soon be nothing left.

Even the most responsible visitors cause problems through their sheer numbers. Archaeologists monitoring Ice Age cave paintings at Lascaux, in France, and wall paintings in the tombs of the pharaohs in Egypt, noticed that the bright designs were fading. This was caused by moisture breathed out by the thousands of visitors. Lascaux cave was closed in 1963, and the Egyptian tombs may follow.

In the years that come, archaeologists will have to find new ways of involving people in archaeology, without putting remains at risk.

Landmarks in archaeology

This time chart outlines some of the major developments and discoveries in the history of archaeology. Early archaeological excavations were carried out by amateurs, who were really little more than treasure hunters wanting to add new works of art to their private collections, or looters, only interested in selling anything they found. But attitudes, interests and methods have gradually changed over the past 150 years, so that archaeology has developed into the scientific discipline it is today.

Internet links

For links to websites where you can explore museums and galleries around the world, interact with virtual exhibits, view video clips and 3-D images of artifacts and read more about different ancient cultures, go to **www.usborne-quicklinks.com**

6th century BC King Nabonidus of Babylon took an early interest in antiquities. He excavated at the ancient city of Ur, a site that was then already 2,000 years old, and housed his discoveries in a kind of private museum.

14th century AD The Aztec people of Central America dug for artifacts in the ancient city of Teotihuacan in present-day Mexico, which had been abandoned centuries earlier.

14th-16th centuries The Renaissance flourished in Europe. During this period, people became very interested in writings, monuments and art from ancient Greece and Rome. Lorenzo di Medici, ruler of Florence in Italy, was a leading figure of the Renaissance and assembled a huge collection of ancient sculptures and vases.

around 1560 Diego de Landa, a priest, recorded details of the writing system used by the Maya people of Central America. This helped later scholars decipher Maya inscriptions.

around 1675 Carlos de Siguenza y Gongora, a government official in Mexico, dug a tunnel into the Pyramid of the Moon at Teotihuacan to investigate it.

1675 Scholar Antoine Desgodets went to Rome where he systematically measured, drew and described many of the ruins there. His work set standards of observation for the next 100 years.

1683 The Ashmolean Museum was founded in Oxford, England, to house rare objects collected by John Tradescant and his son, and Elias Ashmole. Like other collections of the time, it contained a wide variety of rare objects such as shells and books, as well as ancient artifacts. This was the first public museum in Britain.

1693 Scholar John Aubrey completed, but never published, a book containing carefully measured plans of the standing stones and sites of Avebury and Stonehenge in England, as well as notes on many other ancient sites.

1709-10 The Prince of Elboeuf, a nobleman, dug shafts and tunnels at Herculaneum in Italy. He found the first complete Roman theatre, although he was only really interested in the sculptures he unearthed.

1714 Tsar Peter the Great founded the *Kunstkammer* (meaning "art room"), the first museum in Russia. It contained rare natural specimens and books, as well as ancient artifacts.

1720s August the Strong, Elector of Saxony and King of Poland, founded the Dresden Museum, filling it with rare objects from his own *Kunstkammer*. It was the first public museum to be opened in Germany.

1722 Explorers reached Easter Island in the Pacific Ocean, and were astonished by the huge stone statues they found there.

1724 Scholar William Stukeley published his observations on standing stones and other monuments around Britain, in a book named *Itinerarium Curiosum*. This awakened great interest in ancient monuments around Europe.

1748 The first systematic excavations began at Pompeii in Italy. They were conducted for the King and Queen of Naples, but were really little more than digs for ancient sculptures to add to their private art collections.

1753 Eminent doctor Hans Sloane died, leaving a collection of rare objects to the British people. The British Museum was founded in London to house his collection, which included rare books and natural specimens, as well as some ancient artifacts. More rare books and manuscripts were added later.

1760s onwards Popes Clement XIV and Pius VI founded the Vatican Museum in Rome. It housed many sculptures and artifacts from excavations throughout Italy, as well as art collected by several different popes.

1762 Librarian and scholar Johann Winckelmann wrote about finds at Pompeii and Herculaneum in Italy. This inspired growing interest throughout Europe in Roman art, history and archaeology.

1784 Thomas Jefferson (later US President) excavated a Native American burial mound on his estate in Virginia, USA. Most archaeological excavations at this time were still not being properly recorded, but his work was carried out methodically and systematically.

Lawyer and linguist Sir William Jones founded the Asiatic Society in Bengal, to encourage research into the history, languages and ancient monuments of India. A museum soon followed, to house ancient objects collected by the Society's members.

1785 Scientist James Hutton published *Theory of the Earth*, a book discussing the formation of rocks. This established the principles of stratigraphy - the process by which layers of deposits form in a particular order. These were to form the basis of archaeological excavation in later years.

1790 A massive Aztec statue of the mother goddess Coatlicue was dug up in the main square of Mexico City. A Museum of Natural History was founded, to house Aztec finds from the city alongside other rare objects.

1793 The government of the newly established French Republic founded the Louvre Museum in Paris and opened it to the public. It was formed around the French royal collections of art and ancient artifacts.

1798 A team of scholars accompanied the army of Napoleon Bonaparte to Egypt, and made detailed studies of the many ancient monuments, exotic plants and animals they encountered on their travels. They collected examples to take back to France.

1799 A large block of black basalt stone, dating from 196BC, was found by some of Napoleon's soldiers who were digging for building stones at Rosetta (now Rashid) in Egypt. An ancient Egyptian decree was carved on it, in three different scripts: the Egyptian Hieroglyphic and Demotic scripts, and ancient Greek. It was soon known as the Rosetta Stone, and eventually became the key to deciphering the ancient hieroglyphic script.

1800 Scholar John Frere published an article about his discovery of stone tools in a quarry at Hoxne, in eastern England. He argued that the tools were many thousands of years old, but experts of the time thought humans had not existed that far back, as this did not fit with accounts in the Bible. This sparked an ongoing debate about the real timescale of human history and development.

1812 onwards Scholar and explorer Johann Burckhardt visited the ancient trading city of Petra in Jordan and the ancient Egyptian temple at Abu Simbel, among many other adventures. His journals contained accounts of travels and the many daring disguises he adopted in order to reach these remote areas. They inspired great interest in the languages, ancient monuments and history of Africa and Asia.

1817-19 Circus strongman and entrepreneur Giovanni Belzoni opened up the Pyramid of Chephren at Giza and many previously lost tombs in the Valley of the Kings, in order to sell their contents to collectors. The impressive sculptures he found created great interest in ancient Egypt, but he caused a great deal of damage to ancient monuments and artifacts, including the mummies of several pharaohs.

1819 Doctor and scholar Thomas Young published an article describing his studies of the Rosetta Stone. Although he was not able to identify the language the script represented, and concluded that his approach had been wrong, his research was the first step in deciphering ancient Egyptian hieroglyphs.

1822 Using the texts on the Rosetta Stone, and building on work by Thomas Young, linguist and scholar Jean-François Champollion finally deciphered Egyptian hieroglyphs. He discovered that the language they represented was an ancient form of Coptic, which is still spoken in parts of Egypt today.

1833 Geologist Charles Lyell took up James Hutton's earlier theory when he published a book about geology and rock formation. His ideas did much to prove how far human history stretched back into the past.

1836 Christian Jürgensen Thomsen, curator of the Royal Museum in Copenhagen, decided to arrange displays of prehistoric artifacts according to the materials they were made from, in three separate periods: the Stone Age, Bronze Age and Iron Age. This "Three Age system" soon caught on, as it quickly became clear it was an accurate and useful way of dividing up European prehistory.

1839 Lawyer John Stephens and artist Frederick Catherwood reached the ancient Maya city of Copan in Honduras. Their books about their many expeditions in Mexico brought the monuments of the Maya civilization to public attention.

1841 Amateur archaeologist Jacques Boucher de Perthes published a report describing his discovery of stone tools alongside the bones of extinct animals, in gravel pits on the Somme river in France. This find convinced several leading scholars that human life went back many thousands of years - much farther into the past than most experts had thought.

1843 The world's first professional archaeologist, Jens Jacob Asmussen Worsaae, published a book about the archaeology of Denmark. This was a groundbreaking study as it was the first to tackle the archaeology of a whole region. Worsaae also worked with Christian Jürgensen Thomsen to develop careful methods of excavation that allowed archaeologists to study the relationship between objects in the ground. This helped them determine whether finds from one site were from the same or different periods - a method still used by archaeologists today.

1845-47 Scholar and explorer Austen Layard excavated the remains of Nimrud in modern Iraq. The ancient Assyrian site was stripped of its impressive sculptures, which were sent away to European museums.

1850s onwards Archaeologist Henry Rhind spent two years excavating at Thebes in Egypt,

recording for the first time the precise location of every find. Archaeologists still do this today.

1858 Archaeologist Auguste Mariette was appointed the first director of ancient monuments in Egypt and head of the new museum near Cairo, the first national museum in the Middle East.

1859 Biologist Charles Darwin published a book entitled *On the Origin of Species*. This described his theory of evolution by natural selection and the survival of the fittest. Along with *The Descent of Man*, published 12 years later, this had a profound influence on people's understanding of human prehistory and evolution, though it took many years before these ideas were widely accepted.

1862 The Archaeological Survey of India was set up, to record and study the country's ancient monuments.

A gigantic stone sculpture of a head was uncovered in the Veracruz region of modern Mexico. Archaeologists later found many more examples, and named the ancient people who had made them the Olmecs.

1864 Geologist and archaeologist John Evans published a book on ancient British coins, in which he argued that similar artifacts could be placed roughly in date order by studying developments in their design. This was known as "typology", and became a vital tool for archaeologists. It is still widely used today.

1871 onwards Inspired by legends of the Trojan war, businessman turned archaeologist Heinrich Schliemann excavated the mound of Hissarlik in Turkey, which he identified as Troy. His discoveries caused a sensation, and showed that layers of archaeology at one site could demonstrate how it had changed over time, but he destroyed a great deal of archaeological evidence.

Explorer Karl Mauch arrived at the ancient African ruins of Great Zimbabwe. Although he identified it wrongly as the Palace of the Queen of Sheba (a figure mentioned in the Bible), he awakened interest in the archaeology of Africa.

1875 onwards Landowner Don Marcelino de Sautuola found paintings of animals on the walls of caves at Altamira in northern Spain. He believed they were extremely old, as they looked similar in style to Ice Age carvings, but experts of the time disagreed. Later dating methods showed the paintings were made in the Ice Age, between 13,000 and 11,500BC.

1879 The Bureau of American Ethnology was founded in the US, to study Native North Americans and their ways of life. The Bureau also organized archaeological investigations into many Native American sites.

1880s onwards General Augustus Pitt Rivers excavated prehistoric sites on his estate in southern England. While others were still digging to look for attractive artifacts, he recorded everything, to preserve archaeological evidence about the entire site. This is still the goal of archaeologists today.

1882 The Egypt Exploration Fund was established to sponsor archaeological excavations and research in Egypt.

1884 Archaeologist William Flinders Petrie began excavating in Egypt. He insisted on very methodical recording methods and introduced new ways of dating different parts of a site through their relative positions. He was also a strong believer in publishing excavation reports promptly, arguing that this was the only way other archaeologists could find out about new finds.

1896 Archaeologist Max Uhle began detailed excavations at the Inca city of Pachacamac on the central coast of Peru. His work shed new light on the way of life of the Inca people and laid the foundations for Peruvian archaeology.

1899 Archaeologist Robert Koldewey began excavations at Babylon in modern Iraq, inspired by accounts in the Bible. He made many important discoveries, including the foundations of King Nebuchadnezzar's palace.

1899-1935 Archaeologist Arthur Evans discovered evidence of the ancient Minoan civilization on the Greek island of Crete. He found many inscriptions in unknown scripts used by the Minoan and the later Mycenaean people. None of these scripts was deciphered before Evans died; one of them, Linear B, was cracked in 1953.

1911 Historian and explorer Hiram Bingham reached the Inca site of Machu Picchu in Peru, sparking worldwide interest in the archaeology of the Inca civilization.

1913 The foundations of the Aztec Great Temple were uncovered in Mexico City.

1915-29 Archaeologist Alfred Kidder excavated pueblos in southwestern USA. He pioneered region-wide archaeological surveying as a way of understanding the wider historical and geographical context of sites.

1917 Excavations began at the site of Deir el Medina in Egypt. This led to the discovery of a village built for the workmen who had constructed the tombs of the pharaohs in the Valley of the Kings.

1920s The remains of a previously unknown ancient Indian civilization were uncovered in the Indus Valley. The cities of Harappa and Mohenjo-Daro, in modern Pakistan, were excavated, revealing many mud-brick buildings and a type of writing that has never been deciphered.

1922 British archaeologist Leonard Woolley excavated the ancient Sumerian city of Ur, in modern Iraq, inspired by accounts of the city in the Old Testament of the Bible.

Archaeologist Howard Carter discovered the lost tomb of Pharaoh Tutankhamun, packed with rich grave goods. The pharaoh's mummified body was still in place.

1925 Archaeologist Gordon Childe published a book about prehistoric Europe. It set out some ways in which archaeologists could use collections of artifacts to learn about the development of wider cultures and civilizations. Previously, archaeologists had often thought about different sites and artifacts in isolation.

1928 Archaeologist Li Chi began excavations at the Shang dynasty capital of Anyang. He carefully uncovered more than 300 tombs.

by 1930 Tree-ring dating techniques were developed by scientist Andrew Douglass, allowing archaeologists to put an exact date to some wooden finds. Previously, archaeologists could only date finds approximately, by comparing their style or position with other finds, or with ancient historical records.

1937 Dorothy Garrod became Professor of Archaeology at Cambridge University, in recognition of her outstanding excavations at prehistoric sites in the Middle East. She was one of the first woman archaeologists to be officially recognized in this way.

1938-39 An Anglo-Saxon ship burial was excavated at Sutton Hoo in southern England, complete with magnificent gold grave goods.

1940 Ice Age cave paintings were discovered at Lascaux in southern France.

1946-53 Archaeologist Gordon Willey carried out wide-ranging surveys in the Virú Valley, Peru, combining aerial photography with archaeological survey on the ground. He used this information to find out about changing ancient settlement patterns in the area and their relationship to the landscape. This introduced environmental factors into archaeology.

1949 Radiocarbon dating was developed by scientist Willard Libby. This enabled archaeologists to find out the age of certain organic remains by examining their physical properties. Except for tree-ring dating, it had not previously been possible to date finds by scientific means alone. Later, tree-ring dating was used together with radiocarbon to produce even more accurate dates.

1950 The preserved body of Tollund Man was found in a bog in Denmark. Archaeologists were able to reconstruct exactly how he had died and what his last meal had been, by examining his body carefully.

1952 Archaeologist Alberto Ruz Lhuillier discovered the tomb of ancient Maya ruler Pacal the Great at Palenque in modern-day Mexico.

Linguist Yuri Knorozov made advances in understanding the writings of the Maya people.

1952-58 British archaeologist Kathleen Kenyon led excavations at Jericho in Palestine which uncovered the remains of the oldest known town in the world.

1953 Linear B script, the writing of the ancient Mycenaean people of Greece, was deciphered by British architect and linguist Michael Ventris. He proved that the script had been used to write an ancient form of Greek. Earlier scripts found on Crete, including Linear A, used by the Minoan people, have never been deciphered.

1959 Archaeologists Mary and Louis Leakey found fossils of *Australopithecus boisei*, a very early relative of modern humans, in Olduvai Gorge in Tanzania.

1961 Archaeologist George Bass directed the first ever excavation carried out entirely underwater. It investigated a Bronze Age wreck, sunk off the southern coast of Turkey.

1962 Excavations started at the Viking settlement of L'Anse aux Meadows on Newfoundland Island, Canada. These proved that the Vikings had reached North America nearly 500 years before Christopher Columbus sailed to the New World.

Archaeologist René Millon started work on a massive mapping project at Teotihuacan in Mexico. He combined aerial photographs with surveys at ground level, to understand the archaeology and ancient environment of the whole area. The Teotihuacan Mapping Project has continued to the present day, using the latest techniques including magnetometer and resistivity surveys.

1964-68 UNESCO mounted an international rescue operation to move the temples at Abu Simbel, Egypt.

1966 Russian archaeologist Ivan Pidoplichko began excavations at the Ice Age site of Mezhirich in the Ukraine.

1966-1981 Extensive excavations were carried out at the Native American village of Ozette in Washington, USA. The village had been preserved by a series of mudslides.

1967 Excavations began at the Minoan site of Akrotiri on the Greek island now known as Santorini, which had been covered in ash by an ancient volcanic eruption.

1968 Archaeologists Lewis Binford and David L. Clarke both published books arguing that archaeologists should make use of new methods to create a more scientific approach to archaeological remains. They were interested in understanding the wider processes that shaped past cultures. Previously, many archaeologists had concentrated on reconstructing particular historical events that took place at specific sites.

1972 Frozen mummies dating to around 1475 were found at Qilakitsoq in Greenland.

An experimental and archaeological research project was established at Butser in southern England, to recreate an Iron Age farm and study in detail how ancient varieties of crops, animals, tools and housing performed. This has continued to the present day, and has helped archaeologists understand the daily lives of people in the Iron Age in more detail.

1974 onwards An army of ancient terracotta warriors, buried in the tomb of the emperor Qin Shi Huangdi, was excavated at Li Shan in China. This amazing find attracted thousands of visitors, but the site may have to be closed to prevent damage to the ancient remains.

1975 Remains of a mammoth-hunting settlement dating to around 11,000BC were found at Monte Verde in Chile.

1976 The Viking settlement of Jorvik was uncovered in a rescue dig at York in northern England. Archaeologists recovered evidence about the diet and health of its inhabitants from organic finds at the site.

1978 A rich Celtic burial was found at Hochdorf in Germany.

The Theban Mapping Project was launched, to make a thorough survey of ancient Egyptian burials at Thebes and in the Valley of the Kings. It has continued to the present day, and several lost tombs have been located.

1980 Ancient techniques of raised field agriculture, reconstructed from archaeological evidence, were reintroduced in parts of Peru.

1982 The *Mary Rose*, Henry VIII's flagship, was raised to the surface at Portsmouth, southern England, after 437 years on the sea bed.

1984 Archaeologists Margaret Conkey and Janet Spector published an article arguing that traditional approaches to archaeology ignored the role women had played in past cultures. Soon afterwards, many archaeologists began to study evidence from the recent and distant past about women and female activities.

1985 The wreck of RMS *Titanic* was located on the sea bed off the coast of Newfoundland.

1987 A rich Moche burial was found at Sipán, Peru.

1989 Archaeologist Bruce Trigger published a book looking back at the development of different ideas and approaches in the history of archaeology.

1991 A 5,000-year-old man's body was found in mountains on the borders of Italy and Austria. He was nicknamed Ötzi after the Ötztaler Alps where he was found. By using brand-new scientific techniques, archaeologists were able to find out about the man's diet and health, and even pinpoint precisely which valley he had grown up in.

1995 The space shuttle *Endeavour* took satellite pictures of an ancient temple complex at Angkor in Cambodia, hidden in the dense jungle. The images revealed traces of previously undetected remains, including canals and temples.

1996 Underwater archaeologists located remains of parts of the Egyptian city of Alexandria, now beneath the sea, and the nearby cities of Canopus, Heracleion and Menouthis, which had been destroyed by an earthquake in 746.

1999 More than 200 early Graeco-Roman mummies, some with gold masks, were discovered near the Bahariya Oasis in the Western Desert of Egypt. The burial ground, thought to contain over 10,000 mummies in total, may be the biggest ever found.

2001 A flat bronze circle studded with gold, dating from the Bronze Age, was recovered by police. It had been taken from a site near the village of Nebra in Germany, and may have been used as an astronomical calculator.

2003 Remains of Roman emperor Caligula's palace were found next to the Forum in Rome.

A rich Anglo-Saxon burial chamber dating to around 650 was found at Prittlewell in southeastern England.

During the chaos caused by war in Iraq, archaeological sites were looted and many world-famous artifacts went missing from the Iraq Museum.

Glossary

This glossary explains some of the words associated with archaeology that are used in this book. If a word used in an entry has a separate entry of its own, it is shown in *italic* type.

aboriginal An original inhabitant of a country or region whose ancestors existed there from the earliest times.

acropolis Meaning "high city" in Greek, it was a fortified enclosure built on high ground.

adze A tool consisting of a blade attached to a wooden handle, and used for trimming and dressing wood.

amber A clear yellow fossilized resin from coniferous trees, prized as a material for carved ornaments.

amphitheatre Circular or oval building used as an auditorium or arena, with tiers of seats for spectators.

aqueduct A channel or pipe for carrying water over long distances, sometimes on the top of bridges.

archaeological survey The systematic attempt to locate, identify and record the distribution, form and structure of archaeological sites.

archaeology From the ancient Greek for "the study of what is ancient" and means the study of remains from the past using scientific analysis.

artifact A small object created by humans, such as a tool or work of art.

basilica A Roman public building with a large, rectangular central nave and an aisle on each side. It is also the name for a church with a similar design.

bog Soft, wet and spongy ground consisting of rotting vegetation.

Bronze Age One of the three divisions of *prehistoric* time in the *Three Age System*. This period saw the introduction of bronze for tools and weapons. It has different start dates and durations in different parts of the world.

burial shroud A garment or piece of cloth used to wrap a dead body before it is buried.

bushland An uncultivated or sparsely settled area of land covered with trees or shrubs.

calibrate To fix a scale of measurement.

CAT scan Computed Axial Tomography, the process of using computers to generate a three-dimensional image from flat (two-dimensional) X-ray pictures.

charcoal An impure form of carbon made by burning wood in an airtight space. When burned, charcoal produces an intense heat.

citadel A fortification or place of safety such as a walled city built on high ground, or a stronghold within a city.

civilization A human society made up of complex *cultural*, political and legal organizations.

classification The arrangement of archaeological material and data into groups, using various ordering systems.

colonnade A row of evenly spaced columns.

colony A community of people who have settled in a land distant from their own, but who maintain links with their homeland.

Computer Assisted Design The process by which archaeological information is fed into computers to create images that reconstruct collapsed buildings or other features.

conservation The protection and preservation of archaeological remains.

context The position and state an object is in and the earth and other finds around it.

continent One of the earth's large land masses: Asia, Africa, Europe, Australia, North America, South America, Antarctica.

corrode To be eaten away, especially as in the oxidation or rusting of metals.

crop mark A line that appears in farm crops, indicating an archaeological *feature* under the soil.

culture The shared ideas, values and knowledge of a people. In *archaeology* it is used to mean the associated remains, *features* and *artifacts* of particular peoples.

cuneiform Writing system developed in Mesopotamia, using signs made with a wedge-shaped tool to represent objects, ideas or sounds.

custom The long-established habits or traditions of a society.

cylinder seal An ancient *seal* in the form of a small cylinder of stone often carved with symbols and images and used in the Middle East.

decipher To determine the meaning of something, such as an ancient language.

dendrochronology A dating method, also known as tree-ring dating, introduced by 1930. It is based on the fact that trees add an annual growth ring to their trunk and branches. Archaeologists can calculate the age of the tree by counting and measuring the rings and building up a pattern of rings. They can use this information to date timber on archaeological sites.

dig Another name for an archaeological *excavation*.

empire A collection of peoples and territories under the rule of a single person or group of people.

environment External conditions or surroundings, such as the landscape and vegetation of an area.

ethnoarchaeologist An archaeologist who learns about the past by studying living peoples with traditional lifestyles, examining their skills and *customs* in order to throw light on ancient ways of life.

evolution The gradual change in the characteristics of animals and plants over successive generations. In 1859, Charles Darwin published his theory of evolution by natural selection.

excavation A method used by archaeologists for unearthing buried objects from the ground, in order to discover more information about the past. This is also sometimes known as a *dig*.

experimental archaeology A branch of *archaeology* in which controlled experiments are conducted to provide information that will help with archaeological interpretation. Archaeologists do this by creating and using modern replicas of ancient objects, or even breeding ancient varieties of animals and crops.

feature In *archaeology*, a large, human-made object.

figurine A small carved or cast figure.

fire To bake in a kiln or oven to harden clay.

fission-track measurement A dating method for rocks and *artifacts* that contain uranium and are made using extreme heat, such as glass and pottery.

furnace An enclosed oven in which metals are heated.

geologist A scientist who studies the origin, structure and composition of the earth.

glyph A figure, symbol, character or picture that is carved, painted or in relief.

grid A network of horizontal and vertical lines placed over a map, building or archaeological site for locating points, or a network of streets in a town or city.

hieroglyphics The ancient Egyptian system of writing in which symbols or signs are used to represent objects, ideas or sounds. The symbols themselves are known as hieroglyphs.

historical archaeology A branch of *archaeology* combining archaeological methods and written records, which tends to focus on more recent periods.

historical dating Using ancient calendars and written records as a dating method.

Ice Age A period when much of the earth was covered in ice. There have been many such periods over the past 2 million years, the last one ending 10,000 years ago.

ice core A cylindrical sample drilled from ice.

ingot A piece of cast metal, such as gold, silver or copper, often in the form of a small block.

Iron Age The period when iron tools and weapons were used. Iron-working started at different times in different parts of the world. In Europe it was introduced around 1000BC. This is the third of the periods of the *Three Age System*.

Linear A An early form of writing used by the Minoan people of Crete which has never been deciphered.

Linear B A form of writing used by the Mycenaean people of ancient Greece.

linguist A person who is skilled in languages.

longship A long, narrow boat with oars and a square sail used by the Vikings.

lost wax casting A method of casting bronze sculptures or tools. The form is made in wax and wrapped in clay. This is then fired, which melts the wax to leave a cast in the required shape. Molten bronze is then poured into the cast.

magnetometer A device used to detect magnetic variations underground in order to map archaeological *features*.

maiden voyage The first voyage of a ship.

mammoth A large extinct animal of the *Ice Age*, a relative of the elephant.

marine Something found in or relating to the sea.

marsh Low, poorly drained land that is sometimes flooded and is often on the edge of lakes.

mausoleum A large tomb.

minka A traditional Japanese house, made of wood plastered with mud and with a roof of wood, bark or grass thatch.

mud brick A brick made from mud that has been baked or hardened in the sun.

mummy An embalmed or preserved body prepared for burial, especially in ancient Egypt. It was named after the Arabic word *moumiya*, meaning "bitumen", because the tarry liquid that oozes from mummies resembles it.

nomad A member of a people or tribe who move from place to place to find pasture for their animals.

organic Material derived from plants and animals.

palaeoanthropologist A specialized archaeologist who studies the remains and surroundings of early people.

palisade A strong fence made of wooden stakes driven into the ground and used as a barrier against attack.

papyrus A reed used to make a form of paper, also called papyrus. The reed was cut into strips, then pressed and dried to make a smooth writing surface.

parasite An animal or plant that lives in or on another (the host) off which it feeds.

parchment The skin of certain animals, such as goats or sheep, prepared and treated to form a writing surface.

peat A compact, brown material consisting of decomposed vegetation and water.

photosynthesis The process by which plants use energy from sunlight to change water and carbon dioxide into carbohydrates.

potassium-argon dating Method for dating rocks, based on the decay of a radioactive form of potassium to form the gas argon.

prehistory The period relating to human development before the appearance of writing.

probe A slender instrument used to examine the inside of something, such as an underground tomb or body, without having to open it up.

radar A method for detecting the position and speed of a distant object, based on high-frequency radio waves. Also the name for the equipment used.

radiocarbon dating A method developed in 1949 for determining the date of *organic* matter. It is based on the decay of carbon-14, the radioactive form of carbon.

radiation The emission of energy in the form of heat or light.

remote sensing technology Portable equipment used to detect archaeological remains underground.

rescue archaeology A term for field *archaeology* carried out on sites under threat of destruction. The time allowed for the work is often very limited.

resistivity A type of survey used to locate buried archaeological remains using special equipment to measure tiny changes in the way the soil conducts an electric current.

relic Something that has survived from the past, such as a treasured object or *custom*, often associated with religious ceremonies.

ritual The form of a religious or other ceremony.

sacrifice The *ritual* killing of an animal or person as part of a religious offering to a god.

salvage The rescue of ships and cargoes from the sea.

sanitation Water drainage and other measures to preserve public health.

sarcophagus A coffin or tomb, especially one decorated with paintings, carvings or inscriptions.

satellite A man-made object orbiting the earth, moon or another planet and used to transmit scientific information to earth, or for communication.

savannah Open grassland, usually with scattered trees and bushes.

scalpel A small surgical knife with a short, thin blade.

scan To move a beam of light or electrons over the surface of an object.

seal A device, often in the form of a ring or *cylinder seal*, pressed onto wax or clay and attached to a letter or official document, and used as a mark of authentication.

sediment Material that settles or has been deposited by water, ice or wind.

seven wonders of the ancient world The seven structures ancient and medieval scholars considered the most wonderful in the world: the Great Pyramid at Giza, the Hanging Gardens of Babylon, the statue of Zeus at Olympia, the temple of Artemis at Ephesus, the Mausoleum at Halicarnassus, the Colossus of Rhodes, and the Pharos (lighthouse) of Alexandria.

shard A broken piece or fragment of pottery or glass.

shrine A place of worship associated with a person or god or goddess.

smelt To extract a metal from an ore by heating.

smithy The place where metal, usually iron or steel, is worked by heating and hammering.

sonar A communication device using sound waves to determine the location of objects underwater.

species A biological term for a group of related plants or animals that are similar enough to breed together.

standing stone A large block or slab of stone set up as a marker and sometimes placed with others in circles or avenues. In northwestern Europe the majority of standing stones date to the *Stone Age* and *Bronze Age*.

Stone Age The oldest of the divisions of the *Three Age System*, characterized by the use of stone tools and weapons.

stratigraphy The process by which layers of deposits form in a particular order. This provides the basic rules by which the *context* of archaeological materials are constructed and events placed in sequence.

subcontinent A large area of land that forms a distinct part of a *continent*. India is a subcontinent of Asia.

tablet A slab of stone, clay or wood, especially one used for inscriptions.

tattoo A picture or design on skin made by pricking and then staining with an ink.

terracotta A hard, unglazed baked clay.

thermoluminescence dating A dating method for pottery, in which a sample is heated up releasing trapped energy as light. By measuring the strength of the light, scientists can calculate how long ago the pot was *fired*.

Three Age System The system of classification pioneered by Danish scholar Christian Thomsen in the early 19th century. This divided the period of *prehistory* into three main phases: the *Stone Age*, *Bronze Age* and *Iron Age*. Although it has since been modified, this system still remains the basis of classification of European prehistory.

tree-ring dating see *dendrochronology*.

turf The surface layer of a field, consisting of earth containing the grasses and their roots.

typology The *classification* of objects, structures or specimens by dividing them into groups or types according to their styles, material or use. This system of classification works well with pottery types.

underwater archaeology The study and investigation of archaeological sites, deposits and shipwrecks beneath the surface of water in seas, lakes and rivers.

varves Layers of *sediment* laid down by melting glaciers on the edge of lakes.

water table The level below which the ground is saturated with water.

wetlands An area of *marshy* land.

ziggurat A type of rectangular temple tower erected in stepped levels, found in the area of the Middle East known as Mesopotamia.

Index

The page numbers in *italics* show where to find pictures.
Where there are several pages for a particular entry,
numbers in **bold** tell you where to find the main explanation.

Acknowledgements

Every effort has been made to trace the copyright holders of the material in this book. If any rights have been omitted, the publishers offer to rectify this in any subsequent editions following notification. The publishers are grateful to the following organizations and individuals for their permission to reproduce material (t=top, m=middle, b=bottom, l=left, r=right):

Cover © Archivo Iconografico, S.A./CORBIS, (background) © Sandro Vannini/CORBIS; p.1 © Nevada Wier/CORBIS, (background) © Digital Vision; p.2 © Archivo Iconografico, S.A./CORBIS; p.5 © Charles & Josette Lenars/CORBIS; p.6-7 (background) © Digital Vision; p.6 (t) © Digital Vision; p.7 (b) © Archivo Iconografico, S.A./CORBIS; p.8-9 © Yann Arthus-Bertrand/CORBIS; p.8 (t) Courtesy NASA/JPL-Caltech; p.9 (t) © Lester V. Bergman/CORBIS, (b) © Gianni Dagli Orti/CORBIS; p.10 Mark Lewis/Getty Images; p.11 (b) © Roger Wood/CORBIS, (t) © Archivo Iconografico, S.A./CORBIS; p.12 (t) © Scott T. Smith/CORBIS, (b) CM 1983.3-30.1-872/© Copyright The Trustees of the British Museum; p.13 (b) Werner Forman Archive/National Museum of Ireland; p.14 (b) © Gianni Dagli Orti/CORBIS; p.15 (tr) © Mimmo Jodice/CORBIS, (b) © Gianni Dagli Orti/CORBIS; p.16 (t) Werner Forman Archive/Silkeborg Museum, Denmark, (b) © Richard A. Cooke/CORBIS; p.17 (t) PSU ENTOMOLOGY/SPL; p.18-19 (background) © David Keaton/CORBIS; p.18 (t) © Archivo Iconografico, S.A./CORBIS, (br) Werner Forman Archive/The Greenland Museum; p.20 (b) © Bo Zaunders/CORBIS; p.21 (b) © Franck Goddio/Hilti Foundation Photographer: Cristoph Gerigk, (r) akg-images/Erich Lessing; p.22 (t) © Dead Sea Scrolls Foundation, Inc., The/CORBIS, (b) © Richard T. Nowitz/CORBIS; p.23 (t) © Gianni Dagli Orti/CORBIS; p.24 © Skyscan Photolibrary, (m) © York Archaeological Trust; p.25 (b) Courtesy NASA/JPL-Caltech; p.26 (mr) © Field Archaeology Specialists 2004, (b) © Jonathan Blair/CORBIS; p.27 © Lowell Georgia/CORBIS; p.28 (t) © ADU/Reson Offshore Ltd; p.29 (t) © Franck Goddio/Hilti Foundation Photographer: Cristoph Gerigk, (b) © CORBIS; p.30 (t) © Kevin Fleming/CORBIS, (b) © Jonathan Blair/CORBIS; p.31 (t) © Paul Hardy/CORBIS, (br) © Field Archaeology Specialists 2004; p.32 (t) South Australia Museum, (b) © Anthony Bannister; Gallo Images/CORBIS; p.33 (b) Werner Forman Archive; pp.34-35 © CASA, Department of Architecture and Civil Engineering, University of Bath, UK/Royal Academy of Arts; p.35 (b) © Learning Sites 2003; pp.36-37 © Gustavo Tomsich/CORBIS; pp.38-39 (b) © Jonathan Blair/CORBIS; p.38 (m) Werner Forman Archive/Museum of Mankind, London; p.39 (t) © Archivo Iconografico, S.A./CORBIS; p.40-41(t) John Reader/SPL, (background) Daniel J. Cox/Getty Images; p.41 (r) John Reader/SPL; pp.42-43 (background) © Carmen Redondo/CORBIS, (l and r) © Gianni Dagli Orti/CORBIS; p.43 (ml) © Theban Mapping Project; pp.44-45 (t) Royal Geographical Society/Alamy; p.44 (l) Francois Guillot/AFP/Getty Images; p.45 (r) © Paul Almasy/CORBIS; p.46 (b) © Danny Lehman/CORBIS; p.47 (t) © Richard A. Cooke/CORBIS, (b) © Neil Beer/CORBIS; p.48 (l) © Pat O'Hara/CORBIS, (tr) © Dewitt Jones/CORBIS; p.49 © David Muench/CORBIS; p.50 (t) © York Archaeological Trust, (b) Shaun Best © Reuters; p.51 (m) © Richard T. Nowitz/CORBIS, (b) Courtesy of the Association for the Preservation of Virginia Antiquities; p.52 © Jose Fuste Raga/CORBIS; p.53 (b) Werner Forman Archive/Liverpool Museum, Liverpool, (t) Werner Forman Archive/British Museum, London; p.54 (m) © Gianni Dagli Orti/CORBIS; p.55 (tl) © Ronald Sheridan/Ancient Art & Architecture Collection; (br) © Galen Rowell/CORBIS; p.56-57 (background) © Charles & Josette Lenars/CORBIS; p.56 (b) KENNETH GARRETT; p.57 (br) © Bill Ballenberg/Time Life Pictures/Getty Images; pp.58-59 (background) © Jim Zuckerman/CORBIS; p.59 (tr) © Charles & Josette Lenars/CORBIS, (b) Maria Stenzel; pp.60-61 (background) © Kevin Schafer/CORBIS; p.60 (bl) © Gianni Dagli Orti/CORBIS; p.61 (m) © Gianni Dagli Orti/CORBIS; p.62 (b) Werner Forman Archive/Maori and Pioneer Museum, Okains Bay; p.63 (t) Roger Green/Anthropology Photographic Archive/University of Auckland, (b) © Dennis Marisco/CORBIS; p.64 © Penny Tweedie/CORBIS; p.65 (t) © O. Alamany & E. Vincens/CORBIS, (b) © Paul A. Souders/CORBIS; p.66-67 (background) © Kevin Schafer/CORBIS; p.66 (l) © James L. Amos/CORBIS; p.67 (t) © James L. Amos/CORBIS; p.68 (l) © Gianni Dagli Orti/CORBIS; p.69 (t) © Asian Art & Archaeology, Inc./CORBIS, (b) © David Ball/CORBIS; pp.70-71 (background) © Nik Wheeler/CORBIS; p.70 (l) ANE 118871 © Copyright The Trustees of the British Museum; p.71 (t) ANE 121481 © Copyright The Trustees of the British Museum, (b) © Nik Wheeler/CORBIS; pp.72-73 (background) © David Cumming; Eye Ubiquitous/CORBIS; p.72 (l) © Angelo Hornak/CORBIS; p.73 (r) © CORBIS; p.74-75 (background) © Wolfgang Kaehler/CORBIS; p.74 (t) © Charles & Josette Lenars/CORBIS; p.75 (r) © Lowell Georgia/CORBIS; p.76 (ml) © Christie's Images/CORBIS; p.77 (t) © CORBIS, (b) © Michael S. Yamashita/CORBIS; p.78 (b) © Archivo Iconografico, S.A./CORBIS; p.79 (t and b) © Archivo Iconografico, S.A./CORBIS, (m) Andy Chopping/MoLAS; p.80 C. M. Dixon; p.81 (t) © The Natural History Museum, London; pp.82-83 (background) © Virtalis Limited; p.82 (t) © Adam Woolfitt/CORBIS; p.83 (mr) KENNETH GARRETT National Geographic Image Collection; p.84 (t) Yannis Behrakis © Reuters, (m) © Learning Sites 2003, (b) GR West Frieze II, 2-3 © Copyright The Trustees of the British Museum; p.85 (t) PIZZOLI ALBERTO/CORBIS SYGMA, (b) © Peter Guttman/CORBIS; p.86-87 (background) © John and Lisa Merrill/CORBIS; p.86 (r) © Gianni Dagli Orti/CORBIS; p.87 (t) © Sean Sexton Collection/CORBIS; p.88-89 © Andy Liddell for Campbell Fay/Jorvik; p.88 (l) © York Archaeological Trust; p.89 (t) © York Archaeological Trust; pp.90-91 Dave Roberts/SPL; p.92 © Archivo Iconografico, S.A./CORBIS; p.93 (tl) GR 1910.4-23.1 © Copyright The Trustees of the British Museum, (tr) Werner Forman Archive/British Museum, London, (b) © Gianni Dagli Orti/CORBIS; p.94-95 © Gianni Dagli Orti/CORBIS; p.96-97 (background) © Graham Neden; Ecoscene/CORBIS; p.96 (t) © Doug Wilson/CORBIS; p.97 (l) Simon Fraser/SPL; p.98 (t) Gianni Tortoli/SPL; p.99 (t) M&ME 1881,6-24,1 © Copyright The Trustees of the British Museum, (m) ANE136794 © Copyright The Trustees of the British Museum, (b) © Wolfgang Kaehler/CORBIS; p.100-101 © Otto Lang/CORBIS; p.100 (m) © LANDMANN PATRICK/CORBIS SYGMA; p.101 (t) P&EE 1990 1-2 24 © Copyright The Trustees of the British Museum; p.102 © Roger Wood/CORBIS; p.103 (mr) Alexander Tsiaras/SPL, (b) © Atlantic Productions; p.104 (l and mr) Ethno 1898-1 © Copyright The Trustees of the British Museum; p.105 (t) P&EE 2001 9-1 1-10 © Copyright The Trustees of the British Museum, (b) © Reuters; p.106 (t) © The Natural History Museum, London, (b) © MIT Collection/CORBIS; p.107 (tl) © Digital Vision, (tr) © Macduff Everton/CORBIS, (b) P&EE 1930 4-12 1, 2 © Copyright The Trustees of the British Museum; p.108 © Reuters/CORBIS; p.109 (t) Werner Forman Archive/Peabody Museum, Harvard University, (b) © Jeffrey L. Rotman/CORBIS.

Art director: Mary Cartwright
Digital imaging by John Russell.
Additional designs by Helen Wood, Stephen Moncrieff and Andrea Slane.
Picture research by Ruth King.
Cartography by European Map Graphics Ltd.

Cartographic consultant: Craig Asquith.
Small maps by Craig Asquith and Mike Olley.
With special thanks to Atlantic Productions; Centre for Advanced Studies in Architecture, University of Bath; Field Archaeology Specialists; Jorvik; Learning Sites; Reson Offshore Ltd.; Virtalis Ltd; York Archaeological Trust and also to Rachel Firth and Georgina Andrews.